# MEXICO

# A Revolution by Education

by George I. Sánchez

Foreword by Rafael Ramírez

GREENWOOD PRESS, PUBLISHERS
WESTPORT, CONNECTICUT

# FOREWORD

### BY RAFAEL RAMÍREZ

The Julius Rosenwald Fund has on different occasions shown an interest in the educational and racial problems not only of its own country but also of the world as a whole. In 1935, it had the happy thought of studying the new school movement in Mexico *in situ* and of investigating the manner in which this country's revolutionary governments have been removing obstacles in an attempt to secure some measure of social and economic progress for that immense majority of its population that has been living in extreme misery and ignorance.

Mexico has long been a source of preoccupation to the American people. Our cultural backwardness has bothered them and, possibly because of that, they have in the past thought of us as barbarous. Our revolutions have disturbed them and they have, therefore, thought of my country as disorderly and turbulent. Our campaigns against religious fanaticism have irritated them and, for this reason, it has been said that we are heretics. Our efforts to bring about a more equitable distribution of wealth have aroused indignation and the opinion has been expressed that Mexico is headed towards communism. Many other misconceptions concerning my country are widespread in the American Union. Because of that, when a responsible institution decides to make a conscientious investigation as to the true situation in Mexico, we can only congratulate ourselves and look with sympathy and interest upon the development of its study.

The Julius Rosenwald Fund could not have done better

v

than to choose Dr. George I. Sánchez to make the investigation. A distinguished educator, of wide general culture and of a solid professional preparation, Dr. Sánchez is also a man of penetrating social vision and of an enormous capacity for work. With a good command of the Spanish language, an understanding of our race, and a comprehension of our social phenomena, Dr. Sánchez was able to penetrate to the very soul of our people.

In my long professional life I have met and known other American educators who have come with the purpose of studying the social and educational development of my country. They travel through the nation during two or three weeks—too often in the manner of tourists, always over paved highways. They visit schools and villages along the edge of the road and talk chiefly with people of their own nationality or attempt to learn of Mexican life and institutions through the thick veil of interpreters. Returning to their country they feel satisfied with their studies and prepare now a book, now a bulletin, or at least two or three magazine articles describing what they call the social and educational reality of my country. I do not deny that they say many amiable things that are full of sympathy. I do doubt that through a visit made "on the trot" they have been able to acquire a full and clear vision of Mexican life.

*Mexico: A Revolution by Education,* the book in which Dr. Sánchez gathers his observations and formulates his judgments about Mexico, has been developed in another manner. In the first place, his study covered more than half a year and followed a number of earlier visits to Mexico by him and other officers of the Rosenwald Fund. In the second place, he did not travel only over paved roads nor did he visit only two or three schools, but he travelled in all directions—through the valleys, in the mountains, in the forests, and, in general, through all of those corners where there was something new to see or something typical to study. He rode on mules rather than in automobiles, and he lived for weeks at a time in the homes of the *paisanos* in the little villages. In the third place, he was not content to observe only present social realities but, in order to interpret the present properly, he dedicated himself to the study of our historical past in which present realities have their roots. In the fourth place, listening wisely to the soul of our proletarian multitudes, he learned of their hopes and aspirations. Having visited scores of schools and having placed himself in contact with hundreds of rural teachers and with numerous supervisors and directors of large systems of schools, Dr. Sánchez has had the opportunity of obtaining full knowledge not only of the work itself but also of the thought under which the practical action is unfolded.

The plan under which Dr. Sánchez's book was organized appears to me excellent. He makes a vigorous description of the geographic medium as well as of the scene upon which our agitated social life is unfolded. He places in the hands of the spectator the eyeglasses of history, to the end that the reader may perceive with full clarity all the scenes as they succeed one another on the Mexican stage. Finally, he presents our tormented social life such as it is in reality, throwing floods of light upon climactic scenes—the Revolution, the agrarian question, the labour problem, the anti-fanatical campaign, the socialistic education.

Just as the social complexities of Mexico are surveyed wisely, so are her educational problems. Rural education is stressed in the book, as is natural in treating of a country which, like Mexico, is essentially rural and in which more than two-thirds of its population lives and works in the country. In studying the Rural Schools, the Cultural Missions,

the Regional Rural Schools, the Rural Normal Schools, the
Schools of Article 123, and the Centres of Indian Education,
the author saturates his descriptions with kindness and sympathy—but his descriptions are not coated with sentimental-
ity. Those schools are as he describes them—poor, very poor
in economic resources, although, we hope, rich in social and
cultural values.

In discussing the operation and organization of our schools
the author is willing to give first place to vital content even
though this means the temporary neglect of traditional subject matter. In Mexico we are anxious that our rural population modify its rudimentary manner of domestic, social, and
economic life rather than that it should learn to read and
write. We are more interested that this population should be
cultured, taking the word in its precise acceptance, than that
it should be learned. Our rural education, in effect, stresses
work along these cardinal lines: health and sanitation, the
dignifying of domestic life, elevation of habitual occupation,
recreation and satisfactory social living. After these essentials
come those subjects that American educators call "intellectual
skills and tools."

We Mexican educators have not as yet been able to think
seriously as to whether or not our educational philosophy is
good or bad, for we have hardly had time to work with it in
its initial steps. Nevertheless, bent over the task and in view
of the results which we are obtaining, we believe that we are
on the right path. When our peasant population has acquired
a more satisfactory habit and manner of living, it probably
will be time enough for us to change the emphasis in a programme which has been forced upon us primarily by circumstances and popular demand. In the meantime we will
continue to sustain and support this school which we have
created and which cultivates culture. We believe that it is the

only one capable of bringing about progress in the daily life of our peoples and of transforming slowly the cultural and economic life of our socially retarded peasant class to higher planes.

An expression occasionally repeated by the author in this book is the motto unfurled by all the revolutionary governments which have controlled Mexico since 1922: "To educate is to redeem." The Mexican people must be rehabilitated. We have been accomplishing this slowly in our country, chiefly through the medium of our schools, which have increased annually by thousands. We are committed to that education which will redeem our people.

It is my hope, in the interests of my country, that a large part of the cultured American social group may be able to appreciate this book in all its value. It is also my hope that learned American educators who read it will look with cordial sympathy upon the humble Mexican teachers in the work of redemption which they are carrying on. At the moment they are engaged in organizing the multitudes and bringing about their social and economic rehabilitation. Afterwards they will work—possibly by more formal educational methods—to the end that the luminous motto of our old University may be realized: "The spirit will speak for my race."

*Mexico, March* 1936

# A NOTE ON THE AUTHOR

George I. Sánchez is a native of the State of New Mexico. Of Spanish ancestry, members of the Catholic Church, he and his people have lived in the American South-west for many generations. He has had twelve years' professional experience in education in New Mexico; first as a teacher in a one-room rural school, then as a principal and supervisor, later as a college teacher, and finally as Director of Research of the State Department of Education and President of the New Mexico Educational Association. After he graduated from the University of New Mexico, Dr. Sánchez took advanced studies at the Universities of Texas and California, from which he has master's and doctor's degrees.

The study of the educational movement in Mexico was made under a grant from the Julius Rosenwald Fund. This book, however, is not a publication of the Fund. Nor has the Fund attempted to guide or censor the report. It seemed best to give a competent student full and free scope to make the study in his own way and to present his findings and his opinions on his own responsibility.

# CONTENTS

## The Present School Movement

Contents                                        xiii

# LIST OF TABLES

# PHOTOGRAPHS

(BY THE AUTHOR)

Rural Scenes—Guerrero and Morelos

Indians—Tarahumaras and Huicholes

Public Markets—Querétaro

Arts and Crafts—Lacquer Work, Pottery

Village Trades—Tanning, Pottery

School and Community—Mission on Wheels, Peasant Band

Missioners at Work

Rural Teachers at Mission Institute

Federal Rural Schools—Oaxaca and Tabasco

Local Responsibility in School Building—Chihuahua and Zacatecas

School "Annexes"—Puebla

At an *Internado*—Zongozotla

Indian Students—Cleanliness Committee, Domestic Science

School Activities—Carpentry Shop, Fruit and Vegetable Plot

School Gardens—Tabasco

*Setting and Background*

# CHAPTER I

# MEXICAN MÊLÉE

Mexico is old—Mexico is enigmatic. The fusion of Western civilization and the culture of the "bronze races" has been accompanied by oppression, conflict, and a clash of powers. Centuries of unceasing friction, centuries of constant strife for domination and cultural supremacy have instilled in the Mexican an emotional basis for a consuming urge, a fervid drive, and an unreasoning militant groping for a way out. Yesterday's Mexico lives in the Mexico of today and the dawn of each new day sees the progressive unfolding of a new race with a culture that is not Western, nor Indian, but Mexican.

Long before the coming of the Spaniards in 1519 there was conflict, oppression, and clash of powers. The ambitious and warlike Aztecs had conquered the Valley of Mexico and, by dint of military operations and treaties, held sway over a vast portion of central and southern Mexico. Pre-Columbian Mexico seethed with the conflict of cultures. Nahuatl, Maya, Otomí, Mixteco-Zapoteco, Tarasco, Totonaco—each linguistic group, each Indian tribe sought survival and battled for existence. The mêlée that is Mexico is old; it began centuries before the arrival of Hernán Cortés and his intrepid *conquistadores*. Mexico's problems today have roots in the pre-Columbian contacts and conflicts of Indian groups.

The arrival of the whites in the sixteenth century gave a new direction to the Mexican mêlée. The conflict between Spaniard and Indian soon limited the clash for domination and cultural supremacy to one between conqueror and conquered. The old

3

feuds and aspirations of the various Indian groups were relegated to the background and the simplified clash between Western and Indian cultures took their place. For almost two hundred years only this comparatively simple problem was presented and, slowly but surely, the inspired power of Spanish
Church and State swept the Indian to a position of inferiority
and virtual slavery.

The growth of the *criollos*,[1] the Mexican-born Spanish
classes, and the rise of the *mestizos*, the Spanish-Indian breeds,
complicated the problem, obscured the aims in view, and made
chaos of what might have been colonial destiny or national
policy. The *criollo* sought parity with his brethren from Spain,
the *peninsulares* or *gachupines*, who were privileged in business
affairs and in Church and State. The Spanish blood in the
*mestizo* set him apart from Indian life, yet his Indian blood
lowered him in the eyes of the Spaniard. The simple conflict
between Spanish ruler and Indian subject became a vortex of
impassioned thrusts by *peninsulares, criollos, mestizos,* and
*indios*. Added to this chaotic and internecine strife was the
black pall of the conflict between State and Church and the
drain made on Mexican resources by the increasing demands of
Spain.

For more than four hundred years passions have burned or
smouldered. Occasionally a burst of flame has sought to give
direction to the emotional urge for relief. Sometimes a common
enemy has driven Mexicans to make a united effort, but just
for a brief period and only to falter and fall apart, leaving
Mexico but little farther along the road to national unity. The
successful stroke for independence from Spain; the tremendous
loss of territory to the United States; and the repulsion of the

---

[1] The Glossary (page 193) will explain unusual Spanish or Indian words
and phrases. For convenience of the reader, brief parenthetical translations
will seek to clarify terminology not made clear by the context.

French-inducted Emperor, Maximilian, were but temporary stimulants to the flagging national hopes of a strife-torn Mexico. Through all strife there has been evidence only of unrest, of uncertainty, of vague hopes, and of the unfulfilled wish to be free. Always the desire to be free, but never a clear vision as to ultimate national freedom. Always the search for redemption, but never a national consciousness as to wherein redemption lay.

The sporadic brilliance of an Hidalgo, of a Juárez, of a Madero—yes, even of a Zapata and a Villa—in desperate thrusts at restraining shackles, sought to unfetter the hands and the souls of the Mexicans. These efforts, while successful perhaps in an historical sense, were to no immediate avail in freeing Mexico from the chains of national cultural lethargy. The smouldering mass that has been Mexico has lacked unity, has lacked vision. The motley hordes that flocked to the standards of revolt have been driven to arms and rebellion by inarticulate hopes—by a blind and purely emotional search for release. The *pelado* (poor man) wanted lands, the *indio* (Indian) wanted justice, the *cura* (priest) wanted converts and power, the *político* (politician) wanted autonomy . . . the Mexican people did not know what they wanted. In fact, the Mexicans as a People have not existed! That is the crux of the problem that was Mexico—that is the basic cause for the turmoil of yesterday.

Independence from Spain in 1821 severed the legal ties that bound colonial Mexico to a foreign power but it did not sever the bonds of exploitation and oppression. Change in form did not change the kind of malady that afflicted the people and, to all intents and purposes, Mexico remained the "mother of the world and the stepmother of Mexicans."

The armed Revolution of 1910 was a bloody expression of thwarted hopes. It was a magnificent gesture of disorganized intolerance. It was the impatient emotional explosion of a long-suffering people aroused to a frenzied revolt against its inheritance of subjugation, exploitation, and discrimination. This gesture, this explosion, was chaotic and brutal and it left Mexico physically exhausted and prostrate. To its everlasting glory, however, it left Mexicans with a vision, with a great national hope, and with the glimmerings of an insight into the fundamental ills that had plagued them. The Revolution left Mexicans on the road to national recovery. It left them with the courage to embark upon a new voyage, with renewed hopes, in a new day. The indomitable spirit of the Mexican was not crushed. Physically exhausted, he has borrowed vigour from his trials and sufferings to undertake the road to freedom.

The Mexican mêlée arose from intolerance, ignorance, fanaticism, and racial and geographic provincialism. It arose from the myriad clashes incident to the subjugation of the many by a few—from the disorganized cross purposes of a multitude of contacts among a conglomeration of cultures. The Revolution of 1910 brought the mêlée to a climax by submitting the rights and needs of the masses to the test of war and blood. By 1917 the proletariat had achieved its place of recognition and prestige in the Mexican sun. After the bloody Revolution, the people—not the *cura* or the *militar*, not the *patrón* or the *hacendado*—held the destiny of Mexico.

The Revolution did not end with the silencing of guns and the sheathing of swords. The victory of the masses made it imperative that the Revolution continue, for the injustices of the past had made it impossible for the people to seize the fruits which victory normally would have made possible. Reform, redemption, restitution, and retribution could not await the tedious process of evolution. The Revolution had to go on if the shambles of 1910–1917 were not to be in vain.

Zapata's cry of *"Tierra y Libertad"*—"Land and Liberty"—

during the armed revolution finds echo in the present-day peaceful agrarian revolution. The political and economic dominance of the Church has been broken by a forceful application of the inherent right of the State to control national economy and policy. By peaceful revolution Mexico is striving to overcome in the space of a few years the handicaps it has inherited from centuries of neglect.

Neither the gust of a revolution that has passed nor the dreams of a victorious proletariat can overcome the handicaps of the past in the face of the ignorance of the masses. The cry of the Revolution for the enlightenment of the masses, *"Educar es redimir"*—"To educate is to redeem"—struck at the fundamental cause of the Mexican mêlée, ignorance. The major fruit of victory was the recognition of the rights of the *indio*, of the *pelado*, of the *campesino* (peasant), to enlightenment and culture and to the right to participate and belong in a changing social order. Education, formerly the privilege of the few, by virtue of the popular conquest became a national medium of revolution—a fire to forge a Mexican nation.

Rural Mexico, forgotten Mexico—the major fraction of the Mexican populace—has acquired an unaccustomed privilege. New schools have opened their doors to old Mexico. The school of the Revolution is the rural school—*"La Casa del Pueblo"*—"The House of the People." Schools of action, socialistic schools for an inspired proletariat, are waging a cultural revolution that is rapidly bringing order out of what was the Mexican mêlée.

# CHAPTER II

# MEXICO AND MEXICANS

Mexico is blessed—or burdened—with great geographic and climatic variety. In topography and vegetation, in temperature and rainfall, the country presents almost every extreme. Climate and vegetation do not follow the bounds of latitude but vary with altitude and rainfall. Chiapas, extending the farthest south of all the Mexican states, has southern regions with an average temperature of 50°F. which are bounded on the north by dense tropical forests whose average temperature is more than 90°F. and whose rainfall exceeds 100 inches yearly.

The snow-clad summits of the "God Mates"—Popocatépetl, or *"El Popo"* as the volcano is affectionately called, and Ixtaccíhuatl—command a view of the temperate Valley of Mexico, the fertile fields of Puebla, and the semi-tropical lowlands of Morelos. The white summit of Orizaba, the volcano rising almost 20,000 feet above sea level in the rugged Sierra Madre of the east, finds a contrast in the tropical low country of Veracruz at its foot. The northern *mesa central,* or high central plateau, presents vast reaches of arid and semi-arid mountains and plains more than matched by the heat and dryness of Lower California and western Sonora. Extending along the western coast from Sonora in the north into Central America in the south, the Sierra Madre Occidental is joined in south-central Mexico by the Sierra Madre Oriental which rises along the eastern coast. The narrow strip of coastal lowlands, skirting each of these rugged ranges, spreads out in the south-east in the alluvial plains of Tabasco and Campeche.

8

It would seem that her geography presents the most formidable hurdle to Mexico's march towards cultural advancement, but the human diversity is even more perplexing. Energetic activity is wiping out the geographic barriers through extensive road building, a network of telephone and telegraph lines, the radio, and ever-increasing facilities in rail and aeroplane communication. The isolation of many portions of the 760,372 square miles of Mexican territory is being broken down rapidly by modern means of transportation and communication. Only the success of the educational programme, however, can dissolve the bonds of class antipathy and penetrate the veil of traditional provincialism, superstition, and ignorance.

### Indian Masses

The vast number of Indians, with their conglomeration of languages and dialects, would make the most optimistic of educators quail at the thought of an effective national school system. Ranging from the almost extinct Seris and Lacandones, each numbering less than 300, to the Aztecs, or *mexicanos*, who are estimated at more than 2,000,000, the Indian peoples of Mexico today are thought to comprise at least one-fourth of the nation's total population of 16,552,722.

In spite of the history of such groups as the Apaches in Chihuahua and the Aztecs and Tlaxcaltecs in central Mexico, and even though the Coras of Nayarit and the Yaquis of Sonora have never been completely conquered, the Mexican Indian in general is inclined to a life of quiet and peace. It is noted with relief that warlike perversity is not added to the many other handicaps presented by the Indian to an ambitious nationalistic programme!

The Mexican Indian was despoiled of his lands and driven from his traditional home. He was first made the slave-like

ward of the *encomiendas,* the manorial guardianships, and later
the serf in the feudal *haciendas,* the plantations. The *indio* was
oppressed by his masters, by disease, by hunger, and by social
and cultural ostracism. In spite of this, and in the face of un-
friendly circumstances, he has survived. It is no wonder that
occasionally he has unleashed a maniacal fury at his tormentors.
The depredations of the rabble that rallied to the *"Grito de Dolores,"* Father Hidalgo's cry of independence in Guanajuato in 1810, of the *guerrillas* who supported Zapata in his
bloody gesture for "Land and Liberty" in Morelos, and of the
numerous "bandit" uprisings, can be understood in the light of
the exasperating historical background. Failure to achieve freedom from the social, political, and economic handicaps imposed
upon him has left the Indian weary of the struggle. He has
hidden himself in his mountain fastness, crawled into the shell
of small village life, stolidly resisting the thrusts of a culture
that has brought him only sorrow and privation. Left with less
than 20 per cent of the land, forced to labour in the *haciendas*
and mines, reduced to conditions approaching slavery, the
Indian has turned into himself, jealously holding on to the
crumbs that fell his way and furtively preserving his customs
and traditions, his philosophy, his language.

The Mexican Indians are divided into thirteen general linguistic classes. There are forty-nine ethnic groups and a multitude of tribes and family clans which speak many strange
tongues and dialects. Andrés Molina Enríquez,[1] referring to
the classification by Orozco y Berra, lists over five hundred
separate Indian groups! This list probably exaggerates through
duplication and inaccuracies but serves to portray the immensity
of the Indian problem. Scattered through remote forests and

---

[1] Authoritative sources of references and quotations as well as a list of
publications pertinent to my interpretative report are to be found in the
Bibliography.

swamps, in almost inaccessible *barrancas* or ravines, diffused through mountain fastnesses and parched plains or concentrated in more populous centres, the Mexican Indians present a diversity of conditions, languages, and customs. This situation gives ample justification to efforts such as those of the *Internado Indígena*, the Indian Residential School, at Zongozotla in Puebla. There the teachers, some of whom are pure-blood Indians (Totonac, Aztec, Mixtec, and Zapotec), were concerned with the preparation of a multi-lingual dictionary. My good hosts and *compañeros* there illustrated the task as follows:

| *English* | *Spanish* | *Totonac* | *Aztec* |
|---|---|---|---|
| pig | *cerdo* | *pachne* | *pitzot* |
| water | *agua* | *chuchut* | *at* |
| corn | *maíz* | *cuxil* | *yagol* |
| he | *él* | *in* | *llejua* |
| red | *rojo* | *chichiltec* | *xaxnapap* |

The census of 1930 revealed that 15 per cent of the total population spoke Indian languages and that, of this group, only 53 per cent spoke Spanish in addition to the Indian language. The remainder of this group spoke only an Indian tongue! Over one million people without a common medium of expression outside the family clan or tribe! Add to this the isolation of such groups as the Tarahumaras of the dry mountains of Chihuahua, Sonora, and Durango, the Mixes of Oaxaca, and the Lacandones of Chiapas, and one recognizes a cultural task of tremendous proportions. An exotic array of legends and myths, of fetishes and taboos, of rites and feasts, of customs and costumes, is inextricably woven into the life and the language of the Indian. Munching *tamales* among the Totonacas in the northern Sierra of Puebla, drinking *posole* in the swamps of Tabasco, or partaking of the *pinole* of the Tarahumaras of Chihuahua, I have been appalled by the task confronting the rural school. Even the artificial contact furnished by the interpreter's rendition of the Indian dialect into Spanish is sufficient to arouse a sense of the formidable proportions of the problem.

### The Mestizo Movement

Had the Indian remained in his natural state and had the Spaniard succeeded in his policy of separating the white and bronze races by an unbreakable barrier of class distinction, only the relatively simple problem of articulating subject and governing classes would appear today. However, the circumstances of frontier life and four centuries of close proximity between the two races have made racial mixture and cultural confusion inevitable. Since the earliest days of the Conquest, in spite of antipathies and restrictions, the races have mixed. Indian and Spaniard, *mestizo* and *indio*, Spaniard and *mestizo*, Indian, Spaniard and, to a small degree, Negro have joined to produce a *mestizaje*, a mixture that defies all efforts at definite classification. The *mestizo*, incidental product of two clashing cultures, has arisen slowly to assume the dominant role in Mexico.

The *mestizo*, because he is the by-product of the contact between white and Indian, presents the most complicated picture. Not Indian, yet not European, he is not only a fusion of both but gives evidence of being distinct from either. In a manner of speaking, he alone is Mexican for, contrasted with conquered Indian and conquering Spaniard, he reflects all the elements of the strife and the diverse cultures that make the Mexico of today. Despised and ostracized, reflecting the physical and spiritual strength of the Indian and imbued with the vigour and grace of the *conquistador*, he has lifted his head in the midst of negligence and oppression to direct and command the destiny of Mexico. Justo Sierra in his *Manual Escolar de Historia General* has aptly stated:

> The Spaniard despised the Indian infinitely, considering him as a deficient man and as inherently a servant. The *mestizo*, casual product of the dominant and dominated races, he considered capable only of evil, fitted only for theft and homicide. The *mestizo* or half-caste was, nevertheless, the future owner of the country, the future revolutionary, the future author of nationality.

The *mestizo* movement, as the rise of this heterogeneous group may be called for purposes of brevity, permeates all of modern Mexican history. While it has many manifestations and exhibits diverse and often contradictory tendencies, it is essentially a movement for economic and social security—the search of the *mestizos* for a place in the life of the country, a desire to belong. Though the Indian was unfortunate in his servile status and in the loss of the major part of his lands, he possessed a place, mean and distressing as it was, in the order of things. He had kept some of his villages, portions of his ancient communal landholdings, and was part of a homogeneous though subservient culture. He belonged. He could count on the crumbs incident to his exploitation by the superior class and, though he suffered and starved, he was among his kind and was fortified by the pride of race and tradition. The Spaniards, always a small minority of the population, had constituted themselves a superior caste. As a matter of protection and self-preservation, jealous of pre-eminence and privilege, they closed all doors as far as possible against the *mestizos*. The *mestizo* was an unwelcome interloper—he did not belong to either of his parents. While the Spaniard, through a brilliant and courageous conquest, had carved a niche of authority and power for himself, and while the Indian had been relegated to a life of servitude, the *mestizo* could not rule, neither could he serve. He, indeed, was in a limbo of social, political, and economic insecurity. It devolved upon him to nurse the spirit of unrest and rebellion that he might, thereby, make a place for himself in his beloved Mexico.

The Church gave occupation and means of livelihood to many *mestizos*. Many inherited lands from their Spanish fathers and, being closer to the communal pattern of the Indian than to the individualistic character of the Spaniard, soon converted their *haciendas* or tracts into the *rancherías* and *condueñazgos*—the small farms and common ownerships—which still persist. Large numbers returned to a life among the Indians, accentuating an already serious land problem and adding to the spread of a *mestizaje*. Others secured land by means that do not bear close investigation. Still others dedicated themselves to a parasitical roving life or to one of more direct depredation. The problem of an economic location for the *mestizo* arose in early colonial days, contributed largely to the struggles that resulted in independence, provoked the reform movement of the nineteenth century, found rabid expression in the Revolution of 1910, and is carrying through the agrarian revolution which we witness today.

Even a cursory glance over the pages of Mexican history reveals the profound influence of the *mestizo*. The task of colonial administration was made doubly hard by the socially and economically unattached masses of this culturally irresponsible group. The first hundred years of independence saw *mestizo* leaders and groups striving for emergence from the mire that engulfed them. Lending support first to one movement and then another, their experiences as *insurgentes* and *revolucionarios* slowly developed a class consciousness and some degree of unanimity of aspirations. The Revolution of 1910 was, basically, a *mestizo* movement, waged by *mestizos* in the interests of a new deal for the underprivileged in Mexico. Beginning as a negligible minority, the *mestizos* now number over eleven million and have become the moving element in Mexican reconstruction. Making common cause with dissatisfied *criollos*, enlisting Indian support, the *mestizo* has symbolized the struggle that has given rise to revolutionary Mexico. Because of the force of numbers and owing to his position of economic insecurity, he has *had* to make his way—socially, politically, and economically. He, of all the elements in Mexico, is best fitted to attack national problems with sympathetic understanding. He is best prepared to appreciate the need and the full significance of the cultural revolution inaugurated by the rural school.

### Spanish Influence

After this brief exposition of the trials and woes of the *indio* and the *mestizo*, what can be said about the Spaniard—the *gachupín*, the *criollo*, the conqueror? The Spaniard enslaved and exploited, but this has always happened when a dominant nation has encountered a weaker culture. He permitted the lofty ends of "for God and King" to degenerate to an embattled struggle for the economic resources of Mexico which were so essential to Spain's hopes as a leading European nation. Negligence and indifference in attending to the internal problems of her colonies was the inevitable result of Spain's rapid decline as a world power. Local intrigue in Spain, irresponsibility in delegated authority in New Spain, unbridled individualistic enterprise, international and religious complications, historical circumstances—all these willed that Spanish influence in Mexico lead to anguish and turmoil, to rebellion and anarchy.

The carnage of the Conquest, the heartless exploitation of colonial resources, the establishment of class lines and racial barriers, all were but expressions of the attitude and the proc-

esses of a time and of a civilization. It is unfortunate, but under-
standable, that Spanish procedures did not rise above the level
of past and present practices of Western nations. Justification
is impossible, explanation unnecessary. Wholesale indictments
of a people, however, serve only to blind us to achievement
and impede a true conception of the Mexico of today.
There is no point in arguing the relative value of the contributions of Indian, *mestizo,* and Spaniard. There is a point, however, in the recognition of the position in which circumstances
placed these three to evolve a Mexican nation. In the case of
the Spaniard it must be recognized that, for whatever it is
worth and with apologies to the Mayas, the Aztecs, the Incas,
and the Pueblos, he introduced Western civilization to a New
World.

Spanish influence in Mexico must be judged in terms of the
great extent of territory covered and the millions of Indians
involved. The immensity of the task looms greater when the
relatively small number of Spaniards involved is taken into consideration. Ernest Gruening says:

The conquering Hispanic minority superposed its political structure, religion and language on the natives. In the three colonial centuries but three hundred thousand Spaniards, few of them women,
followed the path cut by the *conquistadores* in New Spain.

It is indeed remarkable that a minority group, certainly never
numbering more than two million (probably less than one and
a half million at the peak), should be able to leave lasting im-
pressions among the multitude of hostile peoples and over
such an enormous territory. Yet, from New Mexico and
California in the north to Chiapas in the south, to say nothing
of Central and South America, the imprint of Spain is very
evident. Mexico proper is truly a new Spain. Language and
literature, architecture and art, crafts and industry reflect the

indelible mark of Spanish culture. Mexico's soul may be Indian, but her means and modes of expression are certainly Spanish.

Almost as a matter of tradition the Spaniards and the *criollos* in Mexico have been the landowners, the shopkeepers, the *patrones*. For centuries they have been the vested interests and, consequently, the conservatives. After centuries of isolation among the *indios* and *mestizos,* constantly involved in a struggle for those things the whites consider theirs by right of conquest, the Spaniards and *criollos* look with disdainful doubt upon the reform movements of the indigenous groups. The white man in Mexico has been accustomed to armed revolt. He is confused by the strategy of a peaceful revolution. The sudden loss of his lands to the peasants under the terms of agrarian reform, however just historically, overwhelms him with a feeling of injustice. The mismanagement of his *haciendas* and mills by his former vassals is sacrilege. Labour troubles with proletarian *sindicatos* and *ligas* (labour organizations) bewilder him—particularly when he knows that oftentimes these unions are instigated by professional, self-seeking politicians. He sees unscrupulous *políticos* growing rich in public office, mulcting peasants through fees and contributions, and forming hydra-headed unwieldy offices for labour and agrarian reform. His bitterness is increased by the inefficiency of carpet-bag government and the extremity of hunger and suffering among those who were to be "redeemed." He gets cold comfort when the hungry peasant, exasperated at the practical inconveniences of sudden social and economic change, cries: "We have exchanged one master for a worse one."

In the peninsula of Yucatán I have listened to landowners express serious doubts as to the security promised by the new order. They see the fruits of a lifetime of endeavour, *henequén* fields and mills, wrested from their grasp and given to untutored field hands. They see undesirable agitators in positions of the greatest social and economic importance. Many of them applaud the social ends of the economic rehabilitation of the masses but despair of their achievement in view of existing suffering and demoralization. The landowner's feudal heritage rebels at the thought of placing his fate in the hands of seemingly irresponsible masses. He is exasperated at the practice wherein choice portions of his plantation are distributed among the peasants although fertile uncultivated land is available! The angry wail of this vested interest is the same all over Mexico. In the mines of the north, in the textile mills of Puebla, in the oil fields of Tampico and Minatitlán, whether it be in the growing of corn, bananas, or rice, the march of a revolution inevitably transgresses the tenets and the established interests of the old order.

The privilege of the few is giving way to the welfare of the many. But the element of injustice to the old order is there and no picture of present-day Mexico is complete without some concept of the position in which the march of events has placed the *hacendado*, the *patrón*, be he Spaniard, Indian, or *mestizo*. Some day some one will write at length on the bitter fruits of the Mexican economic revolution. Until then, this small minority of conservatives will be remembered only as sacrifices to a greater good.

Many Mexicans of pure Spanish blood have been converted to the new order of things. In fact, some were among the original instigators of the reform movement. Many of them have lent and are still lending whole-hearted support to the revolution. Mexico's history shines with the exploits of *criollos* and *peninsulares* who have espoused the cause of the masses and have led *indios* and *mestizos* in the fight for freedom, for land, and for justice. The martyred Cura Hidalgo, "Father of his country," and the martyred President Madero symbolize the part played by many *criollos* as they made common cause with such *mestizos* as Morelos, Guerrero, and Calles and with the immortal Zapotec Indian, Benito Juárez. It is not irony of fate that has placed Spanish-Mexicans in the front ranks of the revolutionary movement, side by side with Indians and *mestizos*. The inheritance from a medieval conquest long ago began to break down in light of the fact that Spaniard, Indian, and *mestizo* were becoming Mexican.

The cry of the Mexican proletariat, "Down with the exploiters," is ostensibly directed against the Spaniard and the Spanish-Mexican. He represented the Church; he was, and is, the business man, the manager, and high official. Rightfully or not, he was selected as the embodiment of the forces which made Mexico "the mother of the world and the stepmother of Mexicans." Yet, while he is conservative and is hesitant and unwilling to relinquish his traditional position, he is, after all, Mexican. The recent immigrant from Spain, the capitalistic American, the Englishman, the German, and the Frenchman —the non-Mexican—is really the target for the shafts of politico-economic reform: "Mexico for Mexicans!"

The exploitation of Mexico and Mexicans by foreigners is a matter of history. Ranging from the staggering loss of more than half of her territory to the United States,[2] to unfortunate loans, and to mineral, power, and agricultural concessions, Mexico has too often been the loser in her dealings with other nations and their nationals. Mexicans have not been blameless

---

[2] The territorial losses to the United States were:

| | |
|---|---|
| 1836—Texas and adjacent territory | 362,487 sq. m. |
| 1848–1853—Arizona, New Mexico, California, Colorado, Nevada, Utah, and part of Wyoming | 568,103 " " |
| Total | 930,590 sq. m. |

This loss represents 170,218 square miles more than the present area of Mexico.

in these losses—far from it! The exploits of Santa Anna, of Díaz, and of others bear witness to this. Yet this does not salve the wounds of injured pride nor make up for the alienation of economic resources. While the landed Mexican, the *mestizo* or *criollo* of means and industry, may be the immediate scapegoat of socialistic propaganda, today's leaders of the proletariat recognize the far-reaching implications of their stand against "*los explotadores.*"

## Poverty in Wealth

The racial and geographic contrasts and extremes already noted have their counterpart in an acutely unbalanced distribution of wealth. Dire poverty and destitution is to be found side by side with opulence. Pathetic beggars may be seen everywhere, dogging the footsteps of the passer-by and plying him with cries for alms. The pleas of "*Socórrame, en el nombre de Dios*" ("Help me, in the name of God"), while sometimes misused by professionals, more often denote real need and reflect the chronic hunger of the masses. They hunger for food and they hunger for the means of livelihood—land, a living wage. The establishment of minimum-wage laws, the governmental support and guidance given labour organizations, the government land banks, the public workers' centres and recreative facilities, all indicate the importance assigned to the social and economic problems of the masses by the revolutionary federal government. Hospices for orphans and for the aged and infirm, federal employment of the destitute, and a new spirit of sympathetic public co-operation bespeak a new deal for Mexicans. This may or may not be socialism. It is certainly typical of the communal pattern of Mexican life—the old Indian pattern.

Mexico has been and is rich—rich in minerals, rich in agriculture, rich in lands—but the masses are poor. The wealth of Mexico has enriched a few but, paradoxically, in the process it

*Table I*

## MINERAL PRODUCTION
### 1930 [1]

| Mineral | Value in Pesos [2] |
| --- | --- |
| Silver [3] | $ 83,900,000. |
| Oil | 80,900,000. |
| Lead | 63,500,000. |
| Copper | 59,800,000. |
| Zinc | 34,600,000. |
| Gold | 27,700,000. |
| Total | $350,400,000. |

[1] Data from *México en Cifras*.
[2] The peso was worth about 33¢ in 1930. It is now worth 28¢ (1936).
[3] Mexico produces about 40 per cent of the world's silver.

has impoverished many. The mineral wealth of Mexico is well known, yet in 1932 the Mexican miner received a yearly wage of less than 240 dollars. In the state of Chihuahua, this meant that each miner received less than one-third of the value of the minerals he produced. Another aspect of the same condition is revealed when it is known that, of the total sum invested in the oil industry in Mexico, 52 per cent was American, 41½ per cent was English and Dutch, *5 per cent Mexican,* and 1½ per cent other nationalities.

Mexico is rich in land, but the Revolution was based on the land hunger of the masses. Even today, after agrarian reform has been in effect for many years, this contradictory condition can be observed at first hand. In 1930, less than 2,000 individuals owned one-third of the total area of the country! There were more than 13,000 proprietors of tracts of land of more than 2,500 acres, while more than 375,000 peasants sought to make a meagre living from tracts of less than 2½ acres! In the same year over four-fifths of all private lands (private lands constituted more than three-fifths of the total area of Mexico) was owned by less than 2 per cent of the private landowners. At that time there were 1,831 private tracts of more than 25,-000 acres each! With these conditions in existence it is no wonder that radical steps are taken by the people and by the federal government in seeking to bring about agrarian reforms. It is no wonder that the rural school has recognized and accepted the challenge of Mexico's land paradox.

It would take many volumes to describe and interpret the changes which agrarian reforms are bringing about in Mexico. The subdivision of *haciendas* to give land to the peasants does more than make free farmers of former *peones.* The material results can be measured, but inextricably interwoven in the process are cultural, social, and psychological effects of transcendent significance. In 1933, by virtue of land reforms, nearly

## Table II

### PRIVATE AND COMMUNAL LANDS ANALYSED BY NUMBER AND SIZE OF TRACTS
### 1930 [1]

| Size | Private | | | | Communal | | | |
|---|---|---|---|---|---|---|---|---|
| | Number | | Area | | Number | | Area | |
| | No. | Per Cent | Thousands of Hectares | Per Cent | No. | Per Cent | Thousands of Hectares | Per Cent |
| Less than 1 Hectare [2] | 244,108 | 28.58 | 100.1 | 0.08 | — | — | .9 | 0.01 |
| 1— 50 Ha. | 526,232 | 61.62 | 4,130.9 | 3.35 | 25 | 0.59 | 38.0 | 0.46 |
| 51— 200 " | 45,274 | 5.30 | 4,735.9 | 3.84 | 272 | 6.49 | 300.9 | 3.61 |
| 201— 500 " | 17,054 | 2.00 | 5,646.5 | 4.58 | 870 | 20.77 | 714.5 | 8.56 |
| 501—1,000 " | 7,908 | 0.93 | 5,754.9 | 4.67 | 978 | 23.35 | 7,290.2 | 87.36 |
| 1,001 Hectares and over | 13,444 | 1.57 | 102,881.6 | 83.48 | 2,044 | 48.80 | | |
| Totals | 854,020 | 100.00 | 123,249.9 | 100.00 | 4,189 | 100.00 | 8,344.5 | 100.00 |

[1] Data from *México en Cifras*.
[2] A hectare equals 2.471 acres or .00386 square mile. There are no *ejidos* (communal tracts) of less than one hectare. However, in 1930 there were 130,806 members of *ejidos* whose individual portions of the communal holdings amounted to less than one hectare.

one million peasants had an average of 25 acres of land each. Before most of these peasants became *ejidatarios*, members of an *ejido* or communal tract, they were *peones*, landless. The redistribution of lands by the federal government released them from peonage and put them "on their own." In receiving land, however, they got more than just land. They got freedom, they were imbued with hope, they were placed on the road to cultural redemption. To the sociologist and educator, the economic aspects of agrarian reform in Mexico are only secondary. Self-respect, independence and freedom, promise of social well-being, and cultural enlightenment are first in importance. The magnificent efforts of the rural school are capitalizing the promises of these land reforms.

The Mexicans are an agricultural people, rooted to the land. Two-thirds of the population lives in rural areas. Over 70 per cent of the people who are gainfully employed are engaged in agriculture. The *campesino* is the typical Mexican. Rural life is typical of Mexican life. Rural Mexico, however, has been forgotten Mexico. Professor Rafael Ramírez, speaking before the Progressive Education Association meeting in Mexico City in August 1935, aptly stated:

As a matter of fact, before 1910 no one in Mexico spoke of the existence of that enormous peasant population in spite of the fact that Mexico is essentially a rural country. Some talk was heard of an *unknown Mexico*, or better still of a *barbarous Mexico*, alluding vaguely to *rural Mexico*. It was necessary that a Revolution, whose process has not yet ended, incubate and unfold in order that we should discover that twelve millions of our brothers actually lived in the country in extreme conditions of misery and lack of culture.

The backwardness and lack of culture in rural Mexico cannot be fully appreciated except through direct observation. The Egyptian plough, introduced by the Spaniards four hundred

*Table III*

## AGRICULTURAL AND FORESTAL CROPS
### 1930 [1]

| Product | Value in Pesos (Roughly, 1 peso = 33¢) |
|---|---|
| Corn | $147,000,000. |
| Cotton | 43,300,000. |
| Sugar Cane | 31,800,000. |
| Wheat | 31,200,000. |
| Coffee | 21,000,000. |
| Forestal (exclusive of chicle) | 21,000,000. |
| Beans | 17,200,000. |
| Alfalfa | 16,900,000. |
| Rice | 7,100,000. |
| Other [2] | 48,800,000. |
| Total [3] | $385,300,000. |

[1] Data from *México en Cifras*.

[2] Among these are included oats, potatoes, bananas, *henequén*, and *maguey* (of the *pulque*, *tequila*, and *mezcal* types).

[3] This amount represents 90 per cent of the value of all crops.

years ago, is still in current use; quite commonly without even a makeshift iron blade. The value of the cattle used as beasts of burden (oxen, young bulls, cows) still exceeds the combined value of all horses and mules in the country. Burros are still common beasts of burden in rural areas. The importance of these animals in rural transportation and communication is evidenced by the fact that in 1930 there were over two million burros and only 750,000 mules and less than two million horses —almost as many burros as horses and mules combined!

The backwardness of rural economy suggested by these conditions is also reflected in the mode of life and in living conditions. Food, clothing, and shelter cannot surpass the standard which this backward sort of agriculture sets. Even though the average value of burros is about four dollars, it is very common to see men, women, and children staggering under enormous loads. Social practices and cultural development must of necessity be handicapped by the meagre existence which results from the inefficient utilization of meagre resources.

Mexico is rural and rural Mexico is backward. Therein lies the challenge to Mexico's new schools. The rural school must meet it. However, it should not be understood that the educational problem in the cities is so very different from that in rural areas. While the *campesino*, Indian or *mestizo*, becomes urban by his very migration to the city, he gains little culturally. It is doubtful if he gains economically. Though he may exchange his sandals, *huaraches*, for a pair of shoes if he is fortunate, and by the grace of that act feel himself a new man, he is still culturally poor, possibly poorer than before. He is still a social inferior. The squalor and filth of parts of every large city speak for the privations suffered by the transplanted peasant. Educationally, the problems of the Mexican city are almost as great as those of the country. A budding industrialization, cosmopolitanism, and a faster manner of life add

Table IV

VALUE OF LIVESTOCK
1930 [1]

| Animal | Value in Pesos (Roughly, 1 peso = 33¢) |
|---|---|
| Cattle [2] | $511,900,000. |
| Horses | 60,600,000. |
| Mules | 51,000,000. |
| Burros | 33,000,000. |
| Hogs | 29,500,000. |
| Goats | 22,900,000. |
| Sheep | 16,200,000. |
| Total | $725,100,000. |

[1] Data from *México en Cifras*.

[2] There were 1,800,000 cattle (oxen, young bulls, cows) used as beasts of burden. They were valued at $114,500,000—more than twice the value of all mules and more than the combined value of horses and mules. Comparative average values per head are: mules, 68 pesos; oxen, 63 pesos; cattle, 51 pesos; horses, 32 pesos; burros, 16 pesos.

to the problem and complicate the mechanics of education. They do not change the basic philosophy—a philosophy which must be, and is, grounded on the fact that Mexico is rural. Later we shall see how the rural school has invaded the city, transforming its tempo slowly to the pervading rhythm of rural Mexico.

### Health and Literacy

It is inevitable that the low standard of economic life should have serious consequences in the physical and mental welfare of the masses. Isolation, unstable and uncertain governmental control, a precarious existence, peonage, and all the circumstances which made rural Mexico a forgotten Mexico have left their mark on the people. The table presented here speaks for itself in illustrating health conditions. The lack of medical services and sanitary facilities is distressing. The ignorance of the people as regards health and medical care is even more distressing.

I have seen the natives of Anenecuilco, birthplace of Zapata, in the State of Morelos, drinking water from the irrigation ditches—a water supply seriously contaminated with the sewage and refuse of the hospitals and townspeople of the neighbouring town of Cuautla. Unsanitary open markets, lack of refrigeration, unhygienic homes contribute to the prevalence of disease. The problem in the cities is complicated by the greater density of population. It must be recognized, however, that uncleanliness and disease are the fruits of negligence and ignorance. The federal government today is waging an extensive campaign to stem the ravages of rampant disease. The government, stimulated by the campaign of the Cultural Mission operating in that district, is installing a pipe line that will bring drinking water to Anenecuilco. In the meantime, also with the guidance of the Cultural Mission, the villagers are

*Table V*

# MEXICAN VITAL STATISTICS COMPARED
## 1931

### DEATH RATE FROM CERTAIN INFECTO-CONTAGIOUS DISEASES
*(Rate per 100,000 Population)*

| Disease | Mexico | United States |
|---|---|---|
| Malaria | 157.1 | 2.1 |
| Whooping Cough | 96.1 | 3.9 |
| Dysentery | 77.4 | 2.0 |
| Smallpox | 73.1 | 0.1 |
| Measles | 64.5 | 3.0 |
| Influenza | 46.6 | 26.5 |
| Typhoid | 31.1 | 4.5 |
| Diphtheria | 6.1 | 4.8 |
| Typhus | 6.1 | 0.0 |

### BIRTH [1] AND DEATH RATE
*(Per 1,000 Population)*

| Country | Birth Rate | Death Rate |
|---|---|---|
| Mexico | 43.3 | 25.9 |
| Puerto Rico | 45.3 | 20.4 |
| Japan | 32.2 | 19.0 |
| Argentina | 28.8 | 12.5 |
| Spain | 28.1 | 17.3 |
| Italy (1932) | 23.8 | 14.6 |
| United States | 18.0 | 11.0 |

[1] The rate given for Mexico (43.3) takes account only of *registered* births. The actual rate is certainly higher, as registrations are still very incomplete.

boiling their drinking water. If the masses lack knowledge of even the rudiments of sanitation and of the prevention of disease, it is because their education has been neglected. A new educational system is now seeking to repair the wrongs of the centuries in health as well as in other phases of human living.

Further evidence of the lack of education is to be found in the large number of Mexicans who are unable to read or write. As late as 1930 more than 6,900,000 people over ten years of age were in this condition. This means that 59 per cent of this portion of the population was illiterate. Forty-eight per cent of the children ten to fourteen years of age was illiterate! The percentages are progressively higher for succeeding age levels. While these figures depict a serious condition, they also give evidence of the progress that has been made within recent years. Thirty-five years ago more than three-fourths of the population was illiterate. In 1921, the illiteracy among the people over ten years of age was 66 per cent. Intensive programmes of adult education and the great yearly increases in school enrolments are making their impression.

## The Challenge to the School

All the elements involved in a study of Mexico and Mexicans point to the all-important part which the new schools must play. The field of their activity must have no bounds, for it is not one ill that besets Mexico but many. Traditional pauperism must be replaced by a newer economy. Stupefying ignorance must give way to universal education. Health, literacy, economy, politics, religion, education, agriculture, communication —all are but parts of one great mosaic, a mosaic that has been cemented together by the passage of centuries, by starvation and the spilling of blood, by slavery and exile. It would be a poor peaceful revolution, indeed, that would limit the school to the teaching of the three R's to children. Adult education, road building, street cleaning, farming, health, greater skill in labour—all aspects of individual and state life must find a place in school activities.

The situation which we have examined so hurriedly is the justification for the new schools in old Mexico. Dr. Moisés Saenz, who was one of the early organizers of the present federal school system, summarized the conditions in one of his bulletins on rural education:

This, then, is the human scene upon which the rural school must act: an abrupt and gloomy land, indomitable mountain range, thirsty steppe, sweet plateau, virgin forest, torrential ravine, a provident clime; a people learned in the wisdom of many races, with a memory of many traditions, tired at times, more often with virginal strength; a confused murmuring of strange tongues, kaleidoscopic coursing of lives and customs; a fluid race, flowing constantly, pure here, turbid there; the complex mentality of the Indian, Moor, and Castilian; a strange religion which sprays the pagan petals of the *zempatzúchil* before the Christian cross;) a country of many peoples, united in sentiment, divided in ideas; a soul in the making, and upon this cosmos the gust of a revolution which has passed leaving the boughs of the trees still waving, the leaves of the forest still trembling, and the consciences awakened and awed, lifting their eyes and seeing a heaven upon which a new sun shines. A magnificent scene upon which the rural teacher comes as a product of that community, planted in that ground, awakened also and excited by the same hurricane which upset every one, tremulous by the very desire to become.

# CHAPTER III

# COLONIAL SCHOOLS

THE prevailing ignorance and cultural poverty among the Mexican masses of today is difficult to understand. It appears incredible that a people, subject to Western influences for more than four centuries, should be so backward, so largely uneducated. Why a new start in the educational conquest of Mexico had to await the passage of a revolution can be understood in the light of the failure of earlier schools. In fact, it might well be said that a fundamental cause of the Revolution of 1910 was the very fact that the colonial schools had failed—that the masses were poor, economically and culturally. They were poor because they were ignorant and they remained ignorant because they were poor.

## *Indian Culture*

It is impossible to evaluate pre-Hispanic culture in Mexico correctly or to make comparisons justly. We can only conjecture as to the trend that Indian life might have taken had not the Conquest arrested its development. The accomplishments of the Mayas, of the Aztecs, of the Zapotecs and Mixtecs, and of other Indian groups in what is now Mexico are worthy of considerable study. They had well-developed arts and crafts, they had achieved a high degree of perfection in some sciences, and their economic and political life reflected considerable advancement. No one who has visited the imposing ruins of Chichén Itzá in Yucatán, or who has viewed the exquisite beauties of the crumbling architectural gems of Mitla in the State of Oaxaca, will deny that they reflect a cultural state of an advanced order. Many such monuments to pre-Hispanic society exist. At Palenque in Chiapas, at Monte Albán in Oaxaca, at Teotihuacán near Mexico City, and at hundreds of other places scattered over the entire country one may still examine ancient culture as expressed in art and architecture.

Various estimates are made as to the number of Indians in New Spain at the time of the Conquest. Andrés Molina Enríquez of the National Museum of Archæology, History, and Ethnography places his estimate at more than twenty-five million—more than one and one-half times the present total population of the country. Even though a great number of Indian languages are still spoken, these languages represent only one-fourth of those that are known to have existed—a fact that lends weight to estimates that place the number of Indians in pre-Hispanic times at more than the present total population.

It is an unfortunate misconception that class distinctions in Mexico originated with the Spaniards. This is far from the truth, for Aztec civilization, the dominant force in pre-Hispanic times, was based chiefly on a rigid demarcation of social classes. At the top were those who might be considered the aristocracy: "nobles," military leaders, and priests. The warrior and merchant classes occupied the middle position in the social and economic scale. The great mass of the Indians were relegated to an inferior place which might be characterized as one of servitude and semi-slavery. The inferior status of the Indian masses, noted under the Spanish regime, existed long before the coming of the Spaniard. While it is possible that at first the Indian masses did not gain a great deal by the introduction of Western civilization, it is quite certain that they did not lose a great deal. They had always occupied a miserable and inferior position in life.

Quite naturally, Indian education observed this distinction

between classes and reflected the moving forces of Aztec civilization—war and religion. Two agencies existed for the formal instruction of Indian youth, the *Calmecac* and the *Telpuchcalli*. Both of these schools limited their efforts entirely to the instruction of the children of the nobles and military leaders. The great masses of the children received no formal instruction and were simply left to the care and control of their parents. Primary education was limited to the instruction imparted in the home. This instruction consisted mainly of preparation for the duties which a child was to perform in later life. The boys were taught to become accustomed to rigours of a military life, to carry loads, and to obey implicitly. At the age of six they were sent to the market-place to earn some trifle. Punishment was severe, both for boys and girls. Maguey thorns were used freely to instill obedience; mischievous or incorrigible children were forced to breathe the fumes from burnt *chile*. If the father was a merchant or craftsman, the boy was soon initiated into the calling of his father. The girls were given instruction in domestic duties. They were taught weaving, the grinding of corn, and the preparation of various foods and articles of clothing.

The children of the nobles, who since birth had been dedicated either to war or to the priesthood, entered the *Telpuchcalli* or the *Calmecac* at the age of fourteen or fifteen. Both of these schools adjoined the temples and were under the direction of the priests. They were residential schools and the school life was severed almost completely from family life. At the *Telpuchcalli* the boys were prepared as warriors. The *Calmecac* instructed boys in the practices of religion and in the knowledge of the priests, who were the scholars and men of science of the time. Many of the boys in this latter school remained for life in the service of the priests, or became priests. The majority left to be married and to enter other fields. A separate school, in connexion with the *Calmecac*, trained girls for service in the temples in much the same way that boys were trained in the *Calmecac*. Many of these girls became attached to this service for life, but most of them left to be married. Reference is occasionally made to other schools of a less attractive nature. Centres for the teaching of the dance and of music, of questionable morality even for that time, are known to have existed. These, however, did not compare in importance to the educational programmes of the *Calmecac* and *Telpuchcalli*. It is evident that the only formal or academic education was the one imparted at the *Calmecac*. There the boys learned to read the hieroglyphics, to understand the pictorial historical documents, and to utilize the highly developed astronomical knowledge of the priests.

The conquest of the City of Mexico, centre of Aztec civilization, put an end to indigenous educational activities. The immediate result was that the children of the nobles were placed in the same position that the great masses of the children had always occupied. From the standpoint of art and science, it is unfortunate that the instruction imparted in the *Calmecac* was lost by the conquest. However, as there was no widespread use of a formal system of education, the loss of the temple schools was not serious to the people as a whole. This is particularly true if we recognize the merits of the first schools established by the Spaniards in the New World. Without doubt, the colonial schools surpassed anything the Indians had ever had and, to the careful student of the history of education, they compared favourably with the best schools that had been established in Europe up to that time. The work of the first schools in America anticipated by several hundred years many "modern" principles of education.

## The Spanish Missionaries

In view of the widespread publicizing of the "atrocities" of the military occupation of Mexico by the Spaniards and of the destructive and enslaving activities of the soldiers of fortune, it is difficult to turn public attention to the good that was done and to the advantages that the Indian peoples secured as a result of this conquest. It is true that there were shameless exploiters, brutal and iniquitous men whose sway of power and influence spread like a terrible plague over the land of Mexico. It should be recognized that there were also large numbers of benevolent and humble individuals who were daily sacrificing themselves to instruct, to elevate, and in fact to "redeem" the masses. A great majority of these public servants were those who, almost four hundred years before the Revolution of 1910, preached and practised the motto, "To educate is to redeem." The political and economic controversies that have existed for centuries between Church and State in Mexico need not blind us to the fact that most of what Mexico had of Western civilization prior to 1910 it owed to representatives of the Catholic Church. The educational efforts of the Catholic friars—Franciscans, Augustinians, Dominicans, and others—constitute an inspiring chapter in Mexican history.

One of the first acts of Hernán Cortés after taking Mexico City was to ask the King of Spain to send holy men who would devote themselves to the instruction and conversion of the Indians. He expressed preference for the monastic orders because, as he stated, he doubted the wisdom of employing the secular clergy. His doubts were based on the fact that the secular clergy of his time was accustomed to wealth and opulence and to practices and customs that ill-befitted those who were to dedicate themselves to the salvation of the Indians. Before the Crown of Spain could accede to the request of Cortés, three intrepid educational and religious pioneers arrived in New Spain. These three were the Flemish Franciscans, Fray Pedro de Gante, Fray Juan de Tecto, and Fray Juan de Aora. These three were men of letters and of wide repute as scholars. Fray Pedro de Gante, cousin to Emperor Charles V, and his two companions renounced a life of ease, forsook their friends and relatives in Flanders, and devoted themselves to a life of privation and hardships among strange peoples in a strange land. In their self-imposed lowly position of lay mendicant friars they crossed the ocean and, barefoot and in humble garb, braved the rigours of coastal plain and mountain ranges to arrive in Mexico City in 1523.

## Schools of New Spain

The first school in the New World was established by Fray Pedro de Gante in 1523 at the village of Texcoco. Here the Indian children, Mexico, and the world were introduced to a true "school of action." It is characteristic of the efforts of the educational pioneers of this period that they practised the theory that, in order to teach, the teacher must first be a disciple of his pupils. Fray Pedro and his companions learned the Aztec language. They studied Indian customs and established cordial and friendly relationships with the Indian nobles as well as with the masses. Instruction in this first school was carried on in Spanish and in the Indian (Aztec) language. Fray Pedro made every effort to relate his teachings to the natural life of his students. Through physical activities, through music and processions, by the use of pictorial illustrations and hieroglyphics, and through the medium of their own language, this far-seeing educator made the school as natural as possible for the Indians and made it truly a school of action and a school of the people. In 1526,

Fray Pedro transferred his centre of operations from Texcoco to the City of Mexico proper. There he established the great Indian school of San José in connection with the convent of San Francisco. There he gathered more than 1,000 Indian children to instruct them in arts and crafts, in music, in reading, and in myriad activities. There, two hundred years before Pestalozzi, three hundred years before Froebel, and almost four hundred years before John Dewey, he had an activity school, a school based on current life.

Fray Pedro did not neglect the education of adults or girls. Through his students, assistants, and monitors he was able to reach not only the students housed at San José but the community roundabout and communities many leagues from the capital. He was able to attract large numbers of the children of Indian nobles as well as of the lowest and most miserable classes. The compulsory-education laws promulgated by the Crown of Spain brought to him the sons of Indian leaders from far distant villages and towns. Through his tireless efforts, in spite of financial difficulties and the opposition of government authorities who feared the dangers of an enlightened Indian population, Fray Pedro's endeavours were crowned with success. Even the most rabid opponents of Indian education conceded in 1541 that there were great numbers of Indians who were able to read and write, both in Spanish and in Aztec. So successful was Fray Pedro that Zumárraga, first Archbishop of Mexico, proposed that the Catechism of Christian Doctrine be written and taught in the Indian language "for there are so many of them who can read." As a matter of fact, Fray Pedro had written and used the Catechism in the Indian language and his version was printed and used in many parts of Mexico. Artisans, artists, scribes, and the future leaders and rulers of many Indian communities and districts were trained at San José.

The efforts of Fray Pedro were bolstered by the comparable work of many others who came to New Spain to give service in the cause of Christianity—education and religion. Seven months after Fray Pedro had arrived at Texcoco, twelve Franciscans, sent by the Crown in response to the request of Cortés, arrived to undertake the educational redemption of the Indians. Speaking of these men, the historian, Joaquín García Icazbalceta says:

The first Spanish missionaries . . . were twelve men . . . for millions of children and adults. A difficult situation . . . further aggravated . . . as they had never heard the language of the pupils. . . . These venerable men quickly took over the unknown tongue and then learned others and still others that they encountered; they understood, or better they guessed, the special character of the town; and at one stroke they convert it, they instruct it, and give it succour. . . . They certainly were not ordinary men: nearly all were men of letters . . . they had excelled in professorships and in pulpits . . . some of noble birth . . . three of royal blood. . . . What strutting doctor, what much-honoured professor, would today accept a primary school in an obscure village?

The founding of elementary schools for Indians went hand in hand with the construction of churches. These churches and their schools were scattered through every district of New Spain, from the far-off Kingdom of Saint Francis (New Mexico) in the north, to Guatemala and Honduras in the south—from the Pacific to the Gulf of Mexico. In the midst of millions of Indians and with the difficulties presented by unstable government and by heartless economic exploitation, it is not surprising that not all of these schools were replicas of the schools in the City of Mexico. It would be too much to expect that, like Fray Pedro's school at the convent of San Francisco, these institutions should combine the functions of a primary school, a secondary school, an industrial school, a normal school, a school of good customs, and a school to prepare for family and civic life. They likewise could not all be schools for training in a new economic and civil order, schools of the humble and fine arts, and schools where modern and ancient languages were taught. However, such holy men as Fray Bartolomé de Las Casas—"Protector of the Indians"— Father Vasco de Quiroga, Archbishop Zumárraga, Fray Bernardino de Sahagún, and many others deserve a place alongside of Fray Pedro for their devotion to the cause of Mexican education. The schools which these men inspired and built and for which they gave their lives marked the beginnings of an educational revolution in many parts of Mexico. It goes without saying that the extent to which other schools achieved similar progress depended on the devotion, initiative, and resources of the individual in charge. The large number of successful ventures, particularly during the sixteenth century, is indicative of a general progressive trend in colonial education.

Most of the early schools for the Indians limited their enrolment largely to the children of the nobles. Often, through subterfuge, substitutes for these children were sent by the Indians themselves, and in this and other ways members of the lower classes received the privilege of an education. This brought about the interesting situation that, because of their better preparation, individuals oftentimes rose from the lower classes to become the leaders and rulers of the Indians. While the residential and formal instruction was limited to the upper class, the children of the proletariat were not overlooked completely. Both adults and children were taught in the *patios* of the schools before they went to work in the morning and often in the evenings as well. The resident pupils of the school served as monitors and assistants to the friar or priest in charge. In the same way girls received the rudiments of an education and were instructed in Christian doctrine.

It is important to note that the first efforts of the educational programme were directed to the instruction of the Indians. The rise of a *mestizaje*, however, soon made evident the educational problem of the mixed bloods. To Fray Pedro de Gante goes the credit of first recognizing this problem and it is known that, in connexion with his great school, he had tried to bring together *mestizo* children who had been abandoned by their Indian mothers. Through the efforts of Archbishop Zumárraga and Viceroy Mendoza, the famous school of San Juan de Letrán was founded in 1547 to meet the serious need presented by *mestizo* boys. There was also established, in connexion with this school, the School of Our Lady of Charity for the instruction of *mestizo* girls. These institutions rendered valuable service for many years and the school of San Juan de Letrán soon became not only a primary school but also a secondary and normal school and a preparatory school for the colleges and universities. The instruction of girls had been undertaken before 1530 and was carried on by the school mentioned above and through smaller centres under the direction of pious women sent by the Empress of Spain and by the various orders of nuns who began to arrive shortly after the Conquest. In 1552 it was decreed that Spanish girls were to be received at the School of Our Lady of Charity, this being the first time that any school opened its doors to the legitimate daughters of the Spaniards.

The need for more definite provisions for the higher education of the Indians was met by the founding of the College of Santa Cruz de Tlaltelolco in 1536. This school achieved great success in the training of Indian boys and turned out many illustrious leaders. That the programme of Indian education was well received by the Indians is indicated by their desire for more schools, both of primary and higher grades. Upon the petition of Indian leaders and on their assurance that they would bear the cost of maintenance, the College of San Gregorio was opened for Indians by the Jesuits in 1575. This college continued in existence until the nineteenth century, due largely to the fact that it had been endowed by a prominent citizen in 1683.

The Indians' desire for education is manifested in the large numbers the various schools were able to train. The great churches and monasteries, the aqueducts, and other architectural beauties which we see today in Mexico were made possible by the skill and training received by Indians in the schools. The beautifully carved altars and statues, the interior and exterior decoration of churches, and the skilful products of artists and craftsmen owe much of their beauty to this preparation which made possible the artistic expression of the Indian. There are records which point to a long list of Indian scholars who achieved prominence in the fields of arts and letters. Oftentimes these Indians became professors in the schools and colleges—both Indian and Spanish—serving as teachers for their masters and often excelling them in intellectual endeavours. That the colonial schools failed to westernize all of the Indians completely is not greatly to their discredit, for there were relatively few teachers for the millions of Indians in a formidable land. The teachers in the colonial schools, however, in large measure unfettered the hands and the soul of the Indian who, from prehistoric times, had lived in a state of subjugation, oppression, and misery.

The sixteenth and seventeenth centuries saw the founding of many schools for Indians, *mestizos,* and whites. The work of Father Vasco de Quiroga in establishing hospitals and nursery (foundling) schools near the City of Mexico and in the province of Michoacán, as well as his efforts to create a well-ordered type of communistic village and school, deserves particular mention. Father Vasco de Quiroga, travelling over the province of Michoacán, organized villages, established schools, and interested himself in the welfare of the Indians to such an extent that his memory lives vividly in the minds of Tarascan Indians today. The mere mention of his name to many Tarascos is occasion for the shedding of tears and expressions of devotion and regard for one who lived more than three hundred years ago! Today they take pleasure in pointing to the spot where *"Tata"* Vasco passed in his journeys of service and redemption. It was Vasco de Quiroga who planned and established a communistic school in which economic, social, educational, and agricultural activities were carried out in a small community as if that community were one complete family. His "Ordinances" present in detail the theory and practice of a type of school that was admirably suited to the needs of the time and which, like the school of Fray Pedro, was the precursor and indirect pattern for today's socialistic rural schools.

The Augustinians founded various schools, both in Mexico City and in the towns roundabout. They became centres of learning and contributed to the education of whites, Indians, and *mestizos*. Through the work of these schools and those established by the Jesuits, a good deal was done towards the development of secondary and higher education. The institutions founded by the Jesuits filled the need for schools of instruction for Spanish boys. Through their liberal educational programme, based on the teaching of the humanities (Greek and Latin pagan literature), and through the books that they published, the Jesuits did much to elevate the intellectual life of New Spain. These cultured followers of Saint Ignatius of Loyola (founder of the Society of Jesus) gave employment to many Indians and *mestizos*, giving them, at once, both in-

struction and a means of livelihood. Until their expulsion from
Spain and her colonies (from Mexico in 1767) they continued
rendering great service, particularly through their schools.

The founding in 1551 of the Royal and Pontifical University of Mexico (now the National University of Mexico),
which opened in 1553, added the last rung to the educational
ladder. Advanced schools were soon to be found in various parts
of New Spain. Among these were the University of Guadala-
jara in the present state of Jalisco, a minor university in the
far-off State of Chiapas, secondary schools, schools of art, and
many theological seminaries. The rapid rise of secondary and
higher education attests the efficacy and wide distribution of primary schools. Even after a period of decline had set in during
the latter part of the seventeenth century, advanced schools persisted and primary schools continued to supply large numbers
of pupils who had obtained an elementary education.

The coming of the first printing press to the New World in
1535 and the appearance of the first book published on this
continent in 1536 gave fresh impetus to learning. Unfortunately, the narrow outlook of the Church and the opposition
and indifference of the State prohibited the schools from developing the possibilities opened by the new printing press. The
Inquisition, proscription and censorship of literature and
fields of study, and the limitations presented by the traditional method of religious education (catechetical method) all
weighed heavily against the progressive efforts of the early
schools.

While they did not meet fully the educational need of New
Spain, the colonial schools accomplished a great deal more than
can be evaluated merely by recounting the number of schools
and their graduates. The organization of guilds and brother-
hoods of artisans, the rise of a professional group of private
teachers, the organization and establishment of artistic, liter-

ary, and scientific centres give evidence of the unquestionable social and intellectual results of colonial education. The fact that, prior to 1775, the University of Mexico, the first institution of higher learning in the New World, had conferred more than one thousand doctors' degrees and more than twenty-five thousand bachelors' degrees, and that large numbers had obtained the title of Licentiate, Master of Arts, and similar degrees, indicates the influence of the colonial schools on the life of New Spain.

The failure of the colonial schools was not in that education and culture were not spread but that they were spread too thinly. Therein lies the explanation of why it required a bloody revolution to awaken the Mexican people to the need of universal education and why the sacrifice and devotion of Fray Pedro de Gante, of "*Tata*" Vasco de Quiroga, and of their fellow educational crusaders did not achieve the impossible—the complete redemption of the Mexican masses.

It is well to remember that Mexico was never colonized in the sense that the American Colonies were. New Spain existed not as a field of Spanish settlement but rather as a mandate of the Crown of Spain, to be managed and exploited by those upon whom it wished to bestow its gifts. The strides that the rest of the world was taking in economic fields and in social practices were not reflected here because New Spain was a field for exploitation—not for settlement and colonization. The stringent enforcement of laws and practices which led to a virtual prohibition of immigration and the isolated feudal character of the centres of exploitation left the development of new ideas almost entirely to the limited resources of the Mexicans themselves. Thinking in New Spain became inbred. While there was a constant exchange of clergymen and high officials between Spain and her colonies, it was not to the interest of these men to do much for the masses. Most of these officials came for personal or institutional gain and this gain could be achieved only through the exploitation of servile and ignorant masses. At the same time, the Spaniards in New Spain felt that this land and its resources were theirs by right of conquest and that they could obey or disobey the Crown of Spain at will. Lacking mechanical facilities to carry on their exploitation, and as the source of wealth lay in the land, it was inevitable that the Indian and *mestizo* should bear the weight of the economic development carried on to enrich feudal lords.

While the pre-Hispanic population of Mexico is estimated at more than twenty-five million, in the nineteenth century the total population of Mexico was estimated at less than six million! Reading between the lines of these figures we can see how the great masses of the people would find less and less time to devote to their education and how the Church schools would find it more and more difficult either to attract students or to provide the facilities of an educational programme. The economic resources of the Church, which were stupendous, were dissipated in material improvements of the churches themselves, in the rise of the Church to the pinnacle of political and economic power, and in meeting the increasing demand for wealth by the Crown of Spain and the Church of Europe. The landowners and government officials, by the very fact that their economic and social welfare depended upon a menial class, looked with disfavour upon the efforts of the schools to instruct the people. The bitter struggles for political and economic control between Church and State, between factions within the Church and within the State, and the almost complete lack of interest on the part of a corrupt Church-State government relegated education to an insignificant place.

The chief characteristic of the colonial schools is that they were essentially private enterprises with only meagre encouragement from the government. It was not until late in the eighteenth century that a few State schools were established by royal decree and through the efforts of the last viceroys. It is not to be wondered that the early schools, largely individual ventures of conscientious friars and citizens, fell into a pitiful state towards the close of the colonial period. It is a marvel that they managed to survive in such large numbers, still rendering educational service of a sort in the face of neglect, indifference, and opposition.

## Education after Independence

While the colonial period ended with the independence of Mexico in 1821, colonial education may well be thought of as extending until 1910. In so far as the schools are concerned, the restrictions and obstacles that existed during the days of the colony continued to exist until the new educational movement was inaugurated by the Revolution of 1910. Before proceeding to a brief discussion of the schools of independent Mexico it seems proper to state that the early schools were probably no worse than the schools in other parts of the world at the time and that the chief criticism is that there were not more of them. Priestley, in his book, *The Mexican Nation*, says:

Spanish-American civilization of the colonial period must be contrasted, if justly, only with English-American colonial culture. When this is done, disparities are minimized and discrepancies are found to be less important than popular tradition makes them.

For 300 years Spain was the chief agency in the transmission to America of European culture. Her work in that field deserves warm praise for its depth, breadth, and permanency. The refinements of colonial life which accompanied the conquest were inferior to those of no other colonial agency; they approached closely the excellencies then manifested in European culture itself. They were visible in the developments of education, literature, painting, and sculpture, music and the drama, in architecture, and in social amenities which continue today the happy characteristics of the nations politically descended from the second greatest American colonial power.

If the cultural revolution inaugurated by Fray Pedro and his followers lay dormant after the sixteenth century, it is because the inspiration and model which they furnished was submerged under economic exploitation and political anarchy.

It is gratifying to note that Mexican independence was introduced by one whose endeavours typified the work which we have described as being carried on by the early colonial schools. The cry of independence, *"Grito de Dolores,"* by Father Miguel Hidalgo y Costilla, in September 1810, was an outgrowth of the educational activities which he had been carrying on in his capacity as parish priest in the village of Dolores, in the State of Guanajuato. Like many other conscientious missionaries, he had dedicated his life to lending a helping hand to the common people. At his parish he had established a school which included many of the characteristics of the schools of Fray Pedro de Gante and of Bishop Vasco de Quiroga. Because of his activities in the interests of the common people, Father Hidalgo had incurred the suspicion of Church and government authorities. Also because of his interest in the peoples' welfare, he readily joined with those who were willing to take decisive steps to improve the economic and cultural status of the Mexican through political revolt. The blow struck by Father Hidalgo and his followers, in tne hope of freeing Mexico from the domination of Spain, was a stroke for political freedom and popular rights. Up until the time that independence was achieved in 1821 the whole movement was characterized by open revolt and impassioned attacks against the autocratic and feudal character of the government.

It is important to know that Father Hidalgo was disowned by the Church, executed by the government with the sanction of the Church, and that throughout his campaign as a radical reformer he was thwarted at every turn by the entrenched conservatism of Church, State, and economic interests.

The obstacles presented to education during the first decades of independence were many. The conflicts between Church and State, the turmoil incident to the selection of federal and state officials, the secession of Texas and the war with the United States required all the energies and financial resources that the new nation had at its command. Throughout this whole period and extending up until the time of the Revolution there was no concerted or widespread effort to improve the condition of the common people. Benito Juárez sought to elevate the social and political thinking of Mexico. His term of office, interrupted by the French invasion and the three years of rule under Emperor Maximilian, is a bright page in a history otherwise characterized by corruption and utter disregard for the welfare of the masses.

The death of President Benito Juárez in 1872 ended the career of a far-seeing democratic statesman of high ideals. Following Juárez, and in contrast to his government, General Porfirio Díaz, as President of Mexico, exercised his autocratic dictatorial policies over a period of thirty-five years. This selfish and ambitious ruler, by ignoring and violating all legal procedure, perpetuated himself and his followers in office for this length of time and, through the use of the terrors of his iron fist, brought comparative peace and quiet to the Mexican people. The economic development of the country and the financial status of the government reached heights never before attained. Through land and mineral concessions to foreigners and through a complete devotion to material advantages and a total disregard for Mexican rights and Mexican interests, he was able to delude the world into thinking that Mexico was a nation among nations and that his regime had redeemed the Mexican. There is no denying that the material progress of Mexico owes much to the government of Porfirio Díaz, but it is equally true that the well-being of the masses of the Mexican people was not improved.

As early as 1833 laws for the organization of public education in the Federal District were established and public schools of a sort were encouraged and given a little governmental support. The separation of Church and State under the Republic and the antagonism shown towards the Church and its schools reduced whatever value the Church schools had at that time. The new government recognized education as a function of each separate state and decreed that this education should be a lay education as contrasted with the religious education of the Church. While radical leaders at times were able to triumph over the Church in their quest for State education, it was not easy to establish this principle in the face of the power of the Church and the support given it by the conservative elements in Mexico. Constitutional provisions setting forth the basis for a system of education by the State, abolishing convents and their schools, and appropriating the goods of the Church to finance the activities of the State, while demonstrating the wish that liberal leaders had for a national programme, were not rigidly adhered to and did not result in benefit to the education of the people. The Díaz regime ostensibly sought to reduce the power and privileges of the Church but actually enlisted this strong conservative element to further its own ends. The Church continued as a strong factor in State administration and in the economic life of the various states. Public schools were established by the State, but the basic programme of education was still in the hands of the Church and the public schools received only half-hearted support. Díaz himself was never convinced that good would result from the education of the humble classes. It is to be noted that practically all schools were situated in the cities and towns; rural education received almost no attention.

It must not be thought, however, that schools did not exist during this period. In 1894 there were 19 schools of law, 9 medical schools, 8 engineering schools, 26 theological seminaries, a school of mines (established in 1792), 81 lyceums, 4 schools of fine arts, 4 conservatories of music, several schools of arts and crafts, many primary normal schools, and a large number of elementary schools. This very enumeration, however, points to the inadequacy of the school system in meeting the needs of about twelve million people, particularly when the great majority of these people were in rural areas where schools did not exist.

The public schools that existed made education and the imparting of knowledge an end in itself and in no sense did they relate their instruction to the needs of the country. The instruction was of the most formal type and students left these schools with an artificial culture that in no wise fitted them to improve the condition of the people.

Noteworthy among the efforts to reform the academic sort of education that was imparted by the schools in the nineteenth century were the educational undertakings of the Swiss educator, Enrique C. Rébsamen. He sought to introduce more scientific and practical procedures into the training of teachers and into the elementary school curriculum. Beginning by establishing experimental schools in the State of Veracruz shortly before 1890, he extended his influence to other states and his principles of education found an important foothold in the nation. Because of his advanced thinking and because of his practical accomplishments, Rébsamen is recognized as one of the outstanding educational figures of the nineteenth century and as the one who, more than any one else, introduced modern education into Mexico. It is unfortunate that Rébsamen's efforts had to be limited to the centres of population and that, single-handedly, he could not introduce his reforms to every section of the country. Nevertheless, the contribution that he made to educational thought paved the way for a new approach to education throughout the nation.

## The Educational Heritage of the Revolution

Explanation of the distressing conditions in Mexico at the time of the Revolution is to be found in Church-State controversies, in international complications, and in the fact that, at the time of Mexican Independence, Mexico did not exist as a unified nation but rather as a conglomeration of almost independent provinces, states, and feudal subdivisions. Only after ten years of chaos, at the beginning of the twentieth century, was the Mexican nation able to raise itself from the depths it was in. The blood of the Revolution cleansed the country of many of the festering evils that had beset it for centuries. From it arose a recognition of the rights of Mexicans, of all the Mexicans. Through it the Mexican people were awakened to a realization that "to educate is to redeem" and that, through such redemption, to educate is to govern.

Educationally speaking, the Revolution of 1910 found Mexicans no better off than they were one hundred years before. *Los de abajo*, the masses, were still in a condition of oppression and subjugation. The atrocities which characterized the colonial period still persisted. The enslavement of Indians was still carried on, and the land hunger of the people and their thirst for spiritual freedom were not appeased. After a century of attempts at self-government, Mexico had failed. It had failed because, until 1910, regardless of the fact that Mexico was an independent nation, to all intents and purposes it had not arisen from its medieval stage of feudalism.

The failure of the colonial schools and the schools of independent Mexico was a failure of colonial government and of Mexican government. The humanitarian theories and practices of the educational pioneers did not have the financial and political power needed to overcome indifference and corruption in Church-State government. It required the passage of almost four centuries before the nation was ready to shoulder the responsibility of popular education. It was indeed a great loss that, through inefficient and unstable government, Mexico had to wait that long before it began to capitalize on the contributions of her educational pioneers. The path pointed out in the sixteenth century was the path towards the ultimate redemption of the Mexican masses and the path to a cultural revolution. Directly or indirectly, the colonial schools had set the example and had marked out the course through which the Mexican peoples might become a People. The history of the new schools, in truth, does not begin with the Revolution of 1910. In all fairness and justice, it should be said that the new schools in old Mexico are but a renascence of the old schools in New Spain.

*The Present School Movement*

# CHAPTER IV

# MEXICAN RENASCENCE

THE Revolution has given a new life to Mexico. Mexican culture has been reborn—but, rather than being merely a revival of past achievements, Mexico's rebirth looks to the future for perfection. The decade of civil war seems to have called attention to latent Mexican cultural qualities that have lain dormant for centuries. The new freedom has aroused modes of expression that are strikingly Mexican but that, paradoxically, have no well-defined patterns in the past.

Pre-colonial Mexico interwove artistry with life—particularly in the fields of religion and war. The inherent desire for beauty was given vent in the construction of imposing temples, in the carving of exotic statues and bas-reliefs, in the colourful pageantry of religious ceremony, in the pictorial histories, and in the gorgeous costumes of priests and soldiers. Song and legend formed an intimate part of life. A profound respect for the forces of nature underlay the careful observance of rituals to curry favour with natural phenomena. The Indian associated himself with the plant and animal life of his world and learned to appreciate the beauties of nature.

Colonial Mexico perpetuated the tradition of joining religion and beauty. Christian temples exhibit the marks of the fusion of artistic talent and religious fervour. The monuments to Western religion abound with examples of the fine arts as expressed in sculpture and painting, in architecture and crafts, in pageants and drama, in music and festivals. Radiating from the churches and missions, Mexican art found acceptance in the daily life of the masses as well as in the centres of culture. New Spain turned indigenous talents into newer channels, adding some values and discarding others.

It fell to the lot of independent Mexico to submerge native talent and obscure it in the mad rush for the superficial polish of European forms. A blind devotion to continental masters misled Mexicans into a depreciation of local beauty. The vivid colours of native life, the pathos and tragedy of contemporary society, the timid beauty of the daily existence of humble peoples were cast aside. In their place came foreign artificialities and exaggerations which were glaringly out of place in a country where simplicity of line and directness of expression found a peculiarly pleasing setting in the colourful background of the Mexican milieu. With a few exceptions, Mexican art aped European practices and looked down upon the artistic values around it. Ironically, when Mexico was celebrating the severance of political ties with Europe, it slavishly worshipped European models of beauty and assumed for itself a thin veneer of European education and economics.

The Revolution disillusioned the Mexican. Unencumbered by the restrictions imposed by an artificial society and an unresponsive government, he could look upon the Mexican scene in its true colours. Emerging from a successful struggle against dictation and imposition, the Mexican was free to choose his modes of expression, his subjects, his materials. Mexicans had rebelled against privilege and exploitation. It was unthinkable that they should remain submissive to foreign dictation in artistic endeavours, in economic organization, or in education. It was natural that they should look to the Mexican scene itself for their inspiration.

First through armed force—later through the peaceful revolution—Mexicans have rebelled against their heritage from a feudal socio-economic system. Agrarian reforms, collective bargaining, and co-operative marketing are taking the place of special privilege. A Mexican socialistic economy is rapidly replacing individualistic exploitation of human and material resources. Labour unions, business and industry, individual farmers, agrarian villages, public utilities, and public works are receiving the careful attention and close supervision of a revolutionary government. The renascence in politics and industry has taken social security and nationalism as its guiding principles.

The first and the most typical expression of native art was the spontaneous adoption of Mexican tunes as the campaign songs of the Revolution. The agrarians under Zapata marched to the simple refrain of *"Adelita."* Villa's guerrillas raided to the rhythmic tune of *"La Cucaracha."* The catching simplicity of *"Valentina"* was endeared to the followers of Carranza. Calles adopted *"La Borrachita"* as his 1924 political campaign song. Music was in the soul of the Mexican and, in the newly found freedom by revolution, he turned to native tunes for an overt manifestation of joy. The peasants' humble melodies became fashionable. They were of the people and by the people and, in proletarian revolutionary Mexico, they received popular acclaim.

Romantic ballads describe current events, laud contemporary heroes, deplore foreign fads—in fact, any occurrence of popular interest brings forth a new folk-song of this type. The rural folk-songs are full of gaiety and manifest a deep attachment for rural life. Regional music—played on home-made string instruments, marimbas, etc.—everywhere is stimulated and given prominence. Today, native Mexican music has been accepted as worthy of a place in national art. Noted musicians are collecting, writing, publishing, and playing popular music. For the first time, serious study is being given to this phase of Mexican culture. Yet, it remains a popular art. In the wine-shops and taverns, in the streets, at festivals, and in villages and hamlets, native tunes are played and sung and composed. The street urchins, the *pelados,* the peasants, midst dire poverty, give precious pennies to acquire the printed words to a tune sung by itinerant troubadours.

The birth of a Mexican school of painters whose inspiration comes from the Mexican scene has occurred almost overnight. Before the Revolution, almost no one looked to native subjects for this form of artistic expression. Now, major and minor artists everywhere are engaged in portraying Mexico in all its variety and picturesqueness. Pictorial gems are being found in revolutionary themes, in peasant life, among the Indians, in industry, and in Mexican history. Wherever one goes one finds the products of revolutionary painters, humble and great. A nationalistic movement in painting is leaving market-places, government offices, churches, and other public buildings strikingly adorned with colourful murals and drawings interpretative of Mexico's renascence from colonial feudalism to democratic freedom.

Best known of the Mexican nationalist painters is Diego Rivera, whose fame has spread abroad. With a forceful and even radical stroke, he interprets revolutionary policy and uncompromisingly points the way for further social and economic reforms. Through brazen satire, by contemptuous irony, and with studied exaggeration he becomes the champion of the common herd, faithfully baring the deepest hopes—as well as the bitterest resentments—of the Mexican masses. He is an extreme revolutionary and he delights in propagandizing the reform movement. Not all of his themes are of this nature, however. He is a master of character study—choosing his subjects from among the common people. He paints them in all their pathos and tragedy, their colour and gaiety, their simplicity. He excels with his frescoes, of which he has produced enough for a lifetime of a less prolific artist. At first glance his portrayals are crude, his characters stupid and beastly. Careful study reveals a dynamic force that, through caricature and stolidity, draws the spectator with the irresistible attraction which results from an appreciation of the artist's insight.

Rivera, with all his productivity and popularity, is not the only Mexican master painter. Ciqueiros, Orozco, Goitia, Best-Maugard, Covarrubias—to mention only a few—are important rivals for front rank positions, each in his own manner. Others, less well known, are industriously engaged in portraying Mexico as they see it, quite often producing works of beauty and of penetrating interpretation. Many humbler artists have dedicated themselves to the pleasant task of interpreting Mexico through art and of helping others learn this mode of expression. Children, school teachers, mechanics, business and professional people are finding joy in letting brush, charcoal, and pencil speak for them. Revolutionary Mexico has opened the portals of art to the expression of beauty that before was only felt and that had been repressed by an unresponsive social structure.

The renascence has not been limited to music and painting. The nationalistic rebirth of Mexico has brought about the development of many social and cultural trends that are peculiarly adapted to Mexican life. Village crafts have shown marked growth during the last few years. Indigenous communal patterns are being added to the proletarian social structure sponsored by the Revolution. The place of women in society is assuming a new significance. Whether it be through the elective franchise, through participation in government and business, or through co-education and the opening of educational opportunities to them, Mexican women are achieving a degree of prominence never before experienced. Mexico's political renascence is stressing the civic responsibilities and interrelationships of individuals and groups and is giving rise to a feeling of co-operation and brotherhood.

It is impossible to describe all phases of the Mexican renascence in a single volume. This book is devoted to that part of the new Mexico which is expressing itself through schools. The activities of Mexican education may well illustrate the manner in which a people have discarded outworn practices and traditions and are seeking to recreate a national life along new patterns.

Nowhere is the new forward movement more clearly expressed or more definitely emphasized than in the birth of a nationalistic educational programme. Mexican art is championed by the new schools. The native crafts are an essential part of the total school curriculum. Farming and the enrichment of rural life form the corner-stone of the cultural revolution waged by the new rural schools. Social and economic values are being redefined. Careful distinction is being made between sophistication and culture. The redeeming qualities of popular education form the very bases upon which Mexico is waging a revolution by education.

# CHAPTER V

# THE CULTURAL MISSIONS

THE Revolution of 1910—a people unexpectedly gone berserk! Hate and fear, nursed through centuries of cruel subjugation, were given vent in a sudden rebellion against the old order. Finally despairing of relief from above, a people demonstrated its intolerance and made a bid for recognition. The Mexican masses, with a fond memory of the ideals preached by Hidalgo and Juárez, risked all in a wild rising against the conditions that had denied them freedom. Yet, beneath the chaos of mob violence, the Revolution was a search for peace—a quest for political and economic security. The Mexican volcano erupted in the violent surge of the underprivileged seeking material and spiritual peace. The ideals of the Revolution were founded on the needs and rights of the people and, inevitably, cultural enlightenment had to be one of the corner-stones of popular redemption.

In 1910, the thwarted presidential campaign of the idealist Francisco Madero presaged the doom of oppression. The fall of Díaz and Madero's installation as President of the Republic in 1911 bade fair to place the nation on a new and more promising path. But success was not to be achieved so easily. The conscientious and enthusiastic Madero, champion of popular rights and popular education, was not a "strong man" as an executive. Though he failed to capitalize on his popularity and on his own elevated and progressive thinking in his administrative duties, he served Mexico well in his idealism. He had planted the seed of hope in the minds of the people and his influence did not die when he was murdered in 1913.

From 1910 until 1920 Mexico was in constant upheaval, surging with innumerable military uprisings and continuous civil war. Yet, throughout this period, the ideals of the nation's great men formed a strong underlying current which, slowly but surely, was carrying the Mexican people towards peace. The humanitarian principles voiced by Pedro de Gante and Vasco de Quiroga, by Hidalgo and Juárez, and given new expression by the martyred Madero were and, in fact, are the principles of the Revolution. It is not far-fetched to think that, through their example and their more tangible achievements, they were all a part of the Revolution—a moving force in current reforms. It is significant that all reform movements in Mexico have stressed the importance of popular education. From Bishop Zumárraga and Viceroy Mendoza in the sixteenth century, through Father Hidalgo and President Juárez in the nineteenth century and President Madero in the twentieth century, great reformers have sought popular enlightenment. They have accepted the fact that, if the Mexican masses were to be redeemed from slavery, they first had to be redeemed from ignorance. The Revolution recognized that *"Educar es redimir"*—"To educate is to redeem" and that *"Educar es gobernar"*—"To educate is to govern."

The end of the armed Revolution in 1920 found Mexican schools in a sorry plight. As early as 1912 Madero had proposed a federal system of rural schools, but education remained subject to the doubtful jurisdiction of the several states, of municipalities, and of private enterprise. The schools before 1920 were glaring examples of hidebound formalism and of indifference to the needs of the masses of the people. Here and there, through the initiative of a Governor or of some private citizen, a more progressive type of education was encouraged. On the whole, however, it can be said that education was in a state of stagnation and decay. Rural schools were virtually non-existent—popular education being limited to the formal instruction imparted in town or city schools to a limited number of children of the middle or upper classes. The cry of the Revolution had not yet made an appreciable impression on the cultural agencies of the country.

A Federal Bureau of Education had existed prior to 1910 but a misguided revolutionary belief in "states' rights" and "free municipalities" had resulted in its subordination and had prevented the federal government from exercising any direct influence on existing schools. This tragic situation was relieved when, in 1921, President Obregón established a Federal Secretariat, or Ministry, of Education with José Vasconcelos as Secretary. The first Secretary was an enthusiast for the total cultural aspects of a system of schools for the masses. Imbued with the revolutionary spirit, he held to the thesis that the Indian should be "redeemed" and that the masses should be educated. The nation's experiment with a new programme of schools begins with the advent of Vasconcelos as Secretary of Public Education. The educational awakening inaugurated by him has persisted and the task which he shouldered, much too big for any individual or administration, has been carried on by worthy associates and successors.

The Secretariat of Education, immediately upon its creation, sought to carry forth the mission with which the proletarian spirit of the Revolution had endowed it. As the greatest need existed among the *indios* and *campesinos* in the rural areas—areas to which schools were unknown—it was fitting that the federal programme should begin as a pioneering educational adventure among the Indians and peasants. At the same time, the new programme had to be limited to the materials at hand and to the capacity of the Federal Office for leadership and inspiration. Trained teachers were not available, no definite plan of procedure existed, the schools of the time were useless for example and guidance, and even the mechanical processes of administration were lacking. The new schools were starting "from scratch"—experiments in the great mission of true popular education. In the face of an unfavourable tradition and with only a vague memory of the schools of the people that had existed in bygone days, this missionary venture began with an attack upon illiteracy and with an overwhelming and almost fanatical zeal to make the fruits of the Revolution available to forgotten Mexico—rural Mexico.

## The First Missioner-Teachers

The creation of a few federal rural schools, managed largely by teachers who were woefully unprepared to assume the gigantic task set before them, led to a step that has had far-reaching effects upon the whole character of Mexican education. The very fact that the first rural teachers lacked even the rudiments of normal training led Vasconcelos to name a group of supervising teachers who were given the significant title of *misioneros,* or missioners. The stupendous task of initiating and carrying on the cultural revolution was placed in the hands of this first group of cultural missionaries. In speaking of them, a publication of the Secretariat states:

The first task entrusted to the missioners was that of visiting the rural Indian centres of the Republic, of submitting reports regarding the educational condition of the Indians, of intensifying their campaign against illiteracy, and of concentrating rural teachers in zones where the density of Indian population was the greatest. The missioners were charged with the task of recommending the type of education which should be made available to native groups, of observing their economic condition, of selecting rural teachers, of studying native industries and the ways of encouraging them; moreover, [they were charged with] organizing a permanent exposition of the native products and with co-operating with the agronomists of the Secretariat of Agriculture in the study of lands, of the cultivation of crops, of climate, and of communications and salaries. Even then it was thought that both the missioner and the resident teacher should learn the native language of the group, know the economic conditions of the region, and prepare teachers from among the Indians themselves.

It can be seen that the first *misioneros* were to be administrators, supervisors, teachers, research workers, and philosophers! In effect, their activities were to reflect the aims of the total educational programme of the nation. Without ceremony, they were sent into the field to act in their multiple capacity—placed almost entirely on their own resources in carrying out a cultural revolution.

The trust and responsibility placed in the hands of these pioneers were not undeserved. This is evidenced by the proceedings of the Congress of Missioners which took place in September, 1922. As they assembled in Mexico City for their first convention, they asked that education in Mexico be considered a national social problem, that arable land be given to the schools, and insisted that agriculture was indispensable to the programme of the rural schools. These educational missionaries were directing their thinking along the lines which have given the new schools their objective and socialistic character. They, more than any one else, made the rural schools centres of cultural and social activity.

Naturally, this novel departure from traditional practice did not transform rural Mexico overnight. It was an experiment which needed constant revision and rejuvenation. Even so, by 1924 more than 1,000 federal rural schools, attended by 65,000 pupils, had been created. In five short years the missioners and rural teachers had laid the corner-stone of a new movement. The federal schools were the only ones which had broken away from tradition and which were seeking the manner in which the cultural enlightenment of all the people could be accomplished. In 1926, in addition to these federal schools, there were 6,000 state-supported rural schools and about 1,800 private rural schools. These were known as "rudimentary schools"—schools that sought to make the rudiments of reading, writing, and arithmetic available to the peasants. Their very name is indicative of their inadequacy as schools for the masses of the people. It could hardly be expected that the intellectual rudiments would do much to remedy the miserable cultural and economic conditions of the rural masses. Popularly, these schools were dubbed *"escuelas de peor es nada"*— literally "schools that are little better than nothing at all." The town and city schools continued their routine practices of rigid formalism, as yet not feeling the effects of the new wave of educational reform.

The federal school programme was experimental. It was so in 1921 and it is now. The educative process in Mexico does not follow a fixed administrative plan. It is a revolutionary programme, modified by the needs of each individual community and by the materials at hand, adapting itself to the peculiarities of the occasion that it may be better able to modify existing conditions. Being young, it is highly flexible and plastic. Because of this, and owing to the pressing need for immediate action, the *misioneros* had only the revolutionary spirit to guide them. There was no clear-cut precedent to follow and only improvised resources at their command. They had no funds for buildings or for materials, they supervised a group of inexperienced rural teachers whose training probably averaged less than three years of elementary education, and they worked in communities where schools were unknown. In a very real sense they personified the cultural revolution. The missioners were far more than school inspectors or supervisors. They were educational promoters. They were social opportunists building the temple of culture on the site of ignorance and misery. In a strange region and among strange people, they "sold" education to the *indios* and *campesinos* by entrenching themselves in the good graces of the people, fortified by the knowledge that the slumbering and apathetic masses were finally aroused, thanks to the recent civil war.

The community or one of its humble members parted with a bit of precious land so that there might be a school ground. Through the magnetism of the missionary's zeal, the lowly Indians or peasants were attracted to the construction of the building and, elbow to elbow with the *misionero* and his assistants, they erected a temple to the new idealism. As a matter of course they named the school "The House of the People," a simple name, the result of honest endeavour by a humble people, eager for the fruits of an unknown privilege. Out of his own meagre resources, through the sweat of his brow, and at the cost of time lost from his pressing labours, the peasant built a House for his children, for himself, for his neighbour. This symbol of the peace for which he had striven, this monument to the discovery of forgotten Mexico, *had* to be named *"La Casa del Pueblo."*

In 1925, the *misioneros* were converted into a corps of federal inspectors for the rural schools they had established. Their functions took on a more formal supervising and administrative character and became even wider in scope. The growth in the number of schools demanded a more definite co-ordination of the newly born system of federal rural schools, and the experience of the missioners fitted them admirably for the duties of their new positions. But the need for the peculiar service first rendered by the *misioneros* had by no means ceased to exist. Trained teachers were still unavailable. The schools were growing in number and were reaching into every corner of the country. The federal budget for education was mounting to previously undreamed-of heights. New and more remote regions were being explored and community spirit still needed constant stimulation. Education continued to retain its revolutionary qualities and the need for the services of field strategists was greater than ever.

## The Rise of Cultural Missions

It would have been unfortunate, indeed, had the Secretariat of Education been content with supplying poorly trained teachers to the rural schools and with perfecting an administrative system for their control. With a clear understanding of the problem at hand, this office recognized the merit of the field service which it had inaugurated in 1921. The government of President Obregón, through his Ministry of Education, foresaw the impossibility of carrying on a successful system of schools in a land of contrasts and among divergent people if this programme were to receive guidance and direction only from the offices in Mexico City or from a series of offices in the capital cities of the several states. Teacher-training institutions were not available in sufficient numbers and those that existed as yet had no suitable offerings to prospective rural teachers. It was imperative that some agency be placed in the rural field immediately to give training to the teachers and to stimulate and inspire them in their numerous duties. The rural teacher needed help in constructing school buildings, in formulating the daily programme, in utilizing the garden tract at his disposal, in inaugurating and carrying on a system of adult and community education, in improving health and sanitary conditions. What agency could render such a service? Certainly none of those commonly resorted to in the past nor those in other countries which might have been borrowed or taken for a pattern. It fell to the Mexican government to create a new institution that would meet Mexico's unique requirements. The pattern was being furnished by the *misioneros*, whose chief early weakness lay in lack of proper organization and in the fact that their number was so small. With true insight, the Secretariat of Education sought to remedy these weaknesses and to profit by the experiences of the missioners by c  :.ting the agency that is the most Mexican of the nation's educational institutions and that has become the backbone of rural education in Mexico—the Cultural Mission.

In the fall of 1923 the first Cultural Mission left Mexico City to establish its headquarters at the town of Zacualtipán in the State of Hidalgo. The Mission was under the immediate direction of Professor Rafael Ramírez who was later to become chief of the Department of Rural Education in the Federal Secretariat. Accompanying him there were instructors in soap-mal  :, in tanning, in health and physical education, in agriculture, and in music. Señor Ramírez was chief of the Mission and professor of rural education. Rural teachers from the region roundabout were brought together for an institute and given instruction in the various activities. Every effort was made to arouse the interest of the local citizens and it is a matter of record that the first Cultural Mission achieved substantial results in its teacher-training and community work. Towards the middle of 1924 we find Professor Ramírez directing the second Cultural Mission at Cuernavaca in the State of Morelos. This time his group included an instructor in soap-making, a tanner, two agronomists, a carpenter, and a domestic science teacher. After three weeks of intensive work this Mission was able to present an exposition of its accomplishments, demonstrating its success as the type of agency needed in the rural-education programme.

By the end of 1924, when six Cultural Missions were in the field, these agencies had been accepted as an integral part of

## Table VI

## GROWTH OF CULTURAL MISSIONS

| Year | No. of Missions | Institutes Held | Rural Teachers Attending | States Reached |
|------|-----------------|-----------------|--------------------------|----------------|
| 1923 | 1 | 1 | 147 | 1 |
| 1926 | 6 | 42 | 2,327 | 11 |
| 1930 | 14 | 85 | 2,482 | 19 |
| 1935 [1] | 18 | 75 | 4,494 | 20 |

[1] The Republic has been divided into eighteen zones to each of which is assigned a Cultural Mission. It is planned that these zones be further sub-divided as the number of missions is increased.

the educational campaign. Their functions and methods of procedure have varied from time to time, owing to their exploratory character and to their ability to adapt themselves to changing conditions. A Bureau of Cultural Missions was established in the Federal Secretariat in 1926 with Señorita Elena Torres, a capable and brilliant woman, as first chief. Under her direction the missioners were given further training and administrative direction, and courses for teacher-training were prepared. These courses were offered by the Federal School Directors and Inspectors in the various states to their teachers during the Winter Courses or Teachers' Institutes. Soon the practice of holding the Cultural Mission Institutes in the principal cities of the states was discontinued and the Cultural Missions, like the original *misioneros*, were sent directly into the rural areas to carry on their teacher-training and community work. Instead of seeking to gather teachers in centres foreign to their field of daily work, the Mission now carries its programme to the teachers and establishes its base of operations in a rural school. By this change, the Missions became *"normales ambulantes,"* "travelling normal schools," in a very real sense and in a manner which has added much to their effectiveness.

## The Missions at Work

The two major functions entrusted to the Cultural Missions are (1) the cultural and professional betterment of the teachers in service, and (2) the development of popular enthusiasm leading to the cultural, economic, and social improvement of the communities in which the Missions operate. To satisfy these responsibilities the Cultural Mission must serve as:

1. A training centre for the cultural and professional improvement of teachers.

2. An agency for inspiring the teachers with their socializing responsibilities and with a true conception of the part which they are to play in *changing the social order*. This function involves training teachers in the theory of education, in socialistic philosophy, and in practices for the social and economic rehabilitation of the masses.

3. An agency to supplement the work of the normal schools by offering normal-school courses and giving examinations to those teachers who have not completed their academic work in those institutions.

4. A supervisory body concerned with the total school and community programme of the districts within its zone of activity.

5. A social welfare agency which seeks to bring about an improvement in the social and economic practices of the people.

6. A source of propaganda in behalf of socialistic methods and ideals.

7. A community centre and a clearing house for educative materials on topics related to the economic and cultural needs of the people.

The members of a Cultural Mission are chosen not only for their experience and preparation in their respective fields but also for their enthusiasm and personality—for those subjective qualities that are indispensable in meeting the responsibilities of their multiform tasks. The usual personnel of a Cultural Mission consists of (a) a "chief" of the Mission who attends to the direction and co-ordination of the Mission's work and to the instruction in rural education; (b) a "rural organizer" or agricultural social worker who devotes himself to bringing about improvement in agricultural practices, in marketing, in civic organization, and in the social and economic activities of the peasants; (c) a woman social worker whose interest is directed to the improvement of the homes and of family life; (d) a nurse, trained in midwifery, on whom falls the responsibility of attending to questions relating to health and sanitation and who gives guidance and care to the women of the community; (e) a music teacher, to provide for instruction in this field and for the organization and presentation of music festivals by the teachers and by the peasants; (f) a teacher of plastic arts who attends to instruction in painting and drawing, to other manual arts and crafts, and who has charge of the rural theatre (the open-air theatre, marionette and puppet shows); (g) a mechanic who attends to the operation of the motion-picture machine and interests himself in those activities which are related to his training and experience.

The missioners are usually designated as a "group of experts." As a matter of actual practice, a *misionero* is an individual with some training and experience in his particular field of endeavour and whose outstanding qualification is his complete devotion to the cause and his sympathetic understanding of the people among whom he is to work. There are many individuals available who are far better prepared as "experts" but who, lacking this all-important personal qualification, could not possibly serve as missioners. Oftentimes a missioner, with just a smattering of the techniques of his field, is able to accomplish improvements in rural communities that would do justice to an engineer or to a leading figure in his profession.[1]

---

[1] The Secretariat of Education, aware of academic deficiencies in the personnel of the Missions, from time to time gives additional training to the cultural missionaries. The following is a list of courses offered to the missioners by the Secretariat during a recent reunion or institute:

A. Courses Organized by the Institute of Socialistic Orientation. (This Institute is Mexico's "brain trust"—an agency of the administration for the co-ordination of governmental policy and for socialistic orientation.)

    Socialistic Philosophy
    History of Labour Movements in Mexico and elsewhere
    Mexican Revolutionary Rights
      a. Labour Legislation
      b. Agrarian Legislation
    Proletarian Art and Literature
    History of Religion

Upon the Mission's arrival in the district where it is to operate for eight weeks, a rural school is selected as headquarters. This school continues in session during the entire period, becoming the informal practice and demonstration school for the Institute. For the first ten or fifteen days the missioners devote all their time to becoming acquainted with social and economic conditions, with the various civic and labour problems, with the teachers of the district, and with the total environment of the region. In the meantime they have improvised kitchen and sleeping quarters at the rural school and have set the stage for the Institute. The local rural teacher acts as host to the Mission and, informally, becomes a member of that body.

During this exploratory period the missioners make every effort to interest the peasants in the work of the school and the Cultural Mission. Projects are initiated with the help of the local people. The construction of a teacherage may be begun. A marketing association may be inaugurated. Plans may be

---

Modern Educational Theories
Mexican and International Social and Economic History
Co-operativism
    a. Co-operative Doctrine
    b. The Co-operative Societies of Mexico
    c. The Co-operatives in the School
B. Professional Courses
    Social Sciences in the Socialistic Elementary School
    Function of the Nurse in Rural Communities (for the nurses)
    Rural School Organization and Administration with particular reference to the Socialistic School
    Guidance in the Use of Agricultural Machinery (for the mechanics)
    Organization Procedures and Accounting in Co-operatives
    Theory and Practice of Agrarianism
    Theory and Practice of the Conservation of Natural Resources (forests, game, and fish)
    Theory and Practice of Labour Syndicates and Unions
    General Organization—Study of Rural Enlightenment
    *Ejidos* and Mexican Statistics
    Physical Education

formulated for a community electric-light plant—in fact, the Cultural Mission seizes upon and exploits any and all opportunities for the betterment of the community. One of the first acts is to determine the social and political currents that run beneath the surface of community life in order that the problems which arise from them may be met. The village authorities are persuaded to turn over the local jail or dungeon to the school and, in short order, it is tranformed into an additional classroom or into a community co-operative store.

It is a revelation to watch the missioners at work during this initial stage, to see how much they are able to accomplish in so short a time. In a period of ten or fifteen days the missioners lose their status as strangers, they adapt their dress to local custom, they worm their way into the confidence of officials and citizens, they become accepted members of the community. I was dumbfounded at the complete change that had occurred in *misioneros* whom I had known in Mexico City and who had fitted into the cosmopolitan sophistication. As they worked in the rural village, it was difficult to distinguish them from the peasants of the community. Not only that, but they were so definitely entrenched in the good graces of the *campesinos* that they seemed to know all the gossip and all the problems, small and large, that confronted the individual peasants and the community as a whole.

After the short exploratory period the Mission opens its Institute for the rural teachers of the region. Through the co-operation of the state's Federal Director of Education, who exercises jurisdiction over the Cultural Mission, the rural schools of that section of the state are closed so that the teachers may devote four to six weeks to the intensive programme of the Institute. Some twenty to a hundred rural teachers pack up their bed rolls and a few personal effects, including table utensils, and go to the rural school where the Mission is located. The first problem is that of housing the group. The village, naturally, has no facilities for the proper accommodation of this sudden influx of newcomers. By devious ways these teachers are soon installed in makeshift quarters at the schoolhouse, in the homes of leading members of the community, in the hovels of the peasants, and in the teacherage if one is available. This is a great accomplishment in itself. It involves breaking down local antipathies and animosities and, of far greater importance, it places the peasants and teachers in close relationship for the exchange of ideas of mutual benefit. It is easy to see how this arrangement furthers the general cultural programme. In malarial regions the teachers bring or make proper mosquito nettings for their own use and, through their example and instruction, they encourage the people to use this preventive measure. Dozens of simple improvements are a natural result of this relationship.

### DAILY PROGRAMME OF A CULTURAL MISSION INSTITUTE

(Copy of Programme Posted by the Morelos Mission)

| 6 — 7 | a.m. | — Agricultural Practices |
|---|---|---|
| 7 — 8 | " | — Personal Cleanliness |
| 8 — 9 | " | — Breakfast |
| 9 — 10 | " | — Rest Period and Miscellaneous Duties |
| 3 — 11 | " | — Plastic Arts |
| 11 — 1 | p.m. | — Work in the Community |
| 1 — 2 | " | — Luncheon |
| — 3 | " | — Rest Period |
| 3 — 4 | " | — Music and Regional Songs |
| 4 — 5 | " | — Theory and Practice of Co-operatives |
| 5 — 6 | " | — Sports (teachers) |
| 6 — 7 | " | — Sports (community) |

7 — 8  p.m. — Supper
8 — 9    "    — Tuesday and Thursday—Reading in Rural
Library
— Monday—General Assembly
— Wednesday and Saturday—Community Festival
Friday afternoons, after 3 p.m., shall be devoted to the visitation of the schools and communities in the Mission's zone.

Anenecuilco, Mor., May 20, 1935<br>
(Signed)   José Sánchez<br>
Chief of the Mission

The Cultural Mission utilizes every possible opportunity to carry on its work. It is charged not only with the in-service training of teachers, as we know such training in the United States, but also with an integral type of training that is practical in nature and that involves the missioner, the teacher, the pupil, and the adult member of the community. The missioners seem able to hit upon the problems of greatest urgency and to recognize the peculiar needs of the community and of the teachers. In one stroke they begin to remedy local conditions, train teachers in academic and social work, and arouse the peasants to a more progressive home and community life. They instruct and assist the villagers in ways and means of improving themselves, their homes, their agriculture, their community organization. The Institute, then, is not just a teachers' meeting or a teachers' convention where courses in education are offered. It is an experimental agency for social reconstruction and community rehabilitation, with rural villages and schools as the laboratory and with real life presenting the problems for solution.

It might seem that the work of the Institute would lack reality and effectiveness, that the activities of the mission-

ers and of the teachers would assume superficial characteristics. The short period of time in which the work is carried on
—two weeks for the exploratory period of the missioners and
four to six weeks for the intensive work of the Institute—
would, apparently, make it impossible to achieve much of a
substantial or permanent character. True, many of the reforms
inaugurated are discontinued by the community upon the departure of the Mission. Nevertheless, much has been done.
The example set has pointed out possibilities to the peasants.
Many permanent improvements have been made. The corn-
meal mill, the water wheel with its community electric plant,
a sanitary water system, the improved roads made possible
by the guidance of the Institute—contributions such as these
are a source of community pride and have demonstrated their
value to the people. The newly constructed teacherage has
been the means through which the peasants have been introduced to a new and better type of home. The peasants themselves have given of their time and of their limited resources
to bring about improvements in the village and in the village
school and, from that time on, the people of the village have
become a very definite part of the new activities. They have
constructed an open-air theatre and an athletic field where
they may divert themselves as individuals or as a group.

Peasants who, before the coming of the Mission, thought
only of labouring in the fields from sunup until sundown
and who, when their work was done, turned to the *pulquería*
(wineshop, or saloon) for diversion, now have other pastimes
and newer attitudes. I have seen peasants rushing to finish their
day's work before sundown in order that they might have
a few hours of daylight for a basketball game or for the songs
and dances going on at the schoolhouse. I have watched the
*campesinos* participate in presentations of native songs and

dances and in the other cultural and recreative activities centred in the rural school. They come to the schoolhouse armed with their ever-present *machetes* or their sickles and stand patiently around watching the festivities and waiting for a chance to participate. When his turn comes, the peasant puts up his *machete,* arranges his *zarape* (blanket), tightens his *huaraches,* puts back his straw *sombrero,* and, with a smile,[2] enters into a regional dance, a song, or some athletic contest. In villages, where but a short while before a stranger would not have dared enter, visitors are welcomed with open arms to a transformed community and to a new social order.

The work of the Missions might be measured in terms of courses taught, of roads built, of mechanical achievements, and of meetings held. The intangible accomplishments of the Mission cannot be objectively measured. They must be viewed at first hand to be appreciated—they can be measured only in subjective terms by those who can appreciate the difference between the old order and the new, between colonial Mexico and revolutionary Mexico.

How do the missioners go about their tasks at an Institute? The answer to this question can be made only in general terms. Each Mission and the missioners as individuals have characteristics peculiar to themselves, and the procedures which they use are governed by their own initiative, enthusiasm, and capacity for leadership. In general, each of the missioners gives courses in his field to the rural teachers and holds special classes for those *campesinos* who will come to the school. All the courses are taught in an informal manner—the missioner leading the discussion and giving guidance to his pupils in the co-operative pursuit at hand. In addition to this classwork, the

---

[2] Equivalent among these quiet people to a shout among the more blatant Americans.

missioners carry many "extra-curricular" activities which, in reality, are an inseparable part of an integral curriculum which embraces the whole of village life.

The social workers take groups of teachers into the neighbouring villages to do work of an instructive, constructive, and practical nature. They bring about the organization of cooperatives. They advise and participate in improved types of farming and in the improvement of stock. Through their efforts cattle are fenced off and are no longer permitted to share homes with the villagers. Steps are taken to improve roads and irrigation ditches or to drain swampy ground. The women are given classes in sewing and in other domestic arts and every effort is made to improve home facilities. If the peasants come to the school—so much the better. If they don't—the school will go to them, into their homes, into their kitchens, their barns, and their fields. If the community needs more lands, if it needs government assistance in the installation of an adequate water system, if the people have problems or grievances with regard to the agrarian banks or to the marketing organizations, the social workers organize them so that their petitions to the government may have greater weight and so that there may be a unanimity of opinion among the various elements in the town.

The nurse and her group seek out the problems relating to health and sanitation. They make every effort to introduce better practices among the peasants. The villagers are taught how to make mosquito nettings, how to improvise more sanitary sleeping quarters, how to make water safe for drinking purposes, how to construct toilets, and how to prepare better meals.

The mechanic takes his motion-picture apparatus, his electric-light plant, and sometimes a radio in expeditions into the villages of the region. By means of his material equipment he brings both entertainment and instruction to the people. At the same time, he and those with him are able to carry on a very effective propaganda for the type of culture that the Mission has to offer.

The musician has many more duties than the mere training of teachers and peasants in regional songs or in the use of musical instruments. He organizes bands and orchestras; he puts on musical festivals; he furnishes the music for rhythmic physical-education courses and for the dances.

The physical-education teacher has charge of sports, games, plays, and dances. He arranges for competitive tournaments between villages, breaking down centuries-old feuds and prejudices. Through basketball games, through dances and horse races, the missioner and his helpers weave a co-operative pattern among the people and furnish them with a source of pleasure and relaxation. A district, and eventually a state, athletic association is developed. There is a "promoter" of physical education in the Federal Office of Education in each state and in all federal Rural Normal and Agricultural Schools.

The painter has courses in free-hand drawing and mural painting. He makes his work practical by taking his group into the homes of the peasants and decorating these humble edifices with murals that would do justice to the Palace of Fine Arts in the national capital. The schoolhouse, the open-air theatre, the local arts and crafts—all are a part of the laboratory in which this missioner and his group operate. If the local church is no longer in use as a temple of worship, it is redecorated and made into a village auditorium and meeting-place.

The cultural missioners, as opportunists, take advantage of every opening that presents itself and that is suited to the ends which they would achieve. The means to these ends are very limited. Through improvisation, guided by an ingenuity born only of devotion and faith in their patriotic undertaking, and because of a deep-rooted belief in the ideals of the Revolution, the missioners carry on as the spearhead of a cultural revolution.

At the end of four or six weeks the Institute is brought to a close, examinations in the academic courses are given, and a great festival is held. The festival attracts visitors from the towns roundabout, state and federal officials, leading educators and, perhaps, students from foreign lands. The festival itself is a source of inspiration to those who have laboured so hard to make it possible. The peasant is encouraged by the recognition given by leaders in his state and nation to the achievements of his school and his community. The student-teachers rejoice in the successful demonstration of their phase of the work and turn eager eyes to their own communities where they hope to do as well or better. The missioners look upon the festival as a mark of conquest and conversion and feel that they can go to another village, richer by the experiences which they have had. They also know that when they depart they leave behind them a community to which they can return at any time and be received with open arms—where they may look forward to carrying on the good work which they have got under way so well.

The Institute having ended, the missioners spend a week or ten days in the village clearing up unfinished business and organizing the work that has been started in such a way that the peasants may be able to continue the projects under the guidance and leadership of the local teacher. The few belongings of the Mission—bed rolls, pots and pans, the radio and other equipment of the mechanic, the sewing machine, and a few odds and ends—are put into a car, and the intrepid group of educational evangelists set forth to the next district to select another centre of operations and to begin their task anew.

In this way the Cultural Mission travels over a zone made up of one or more states. In the course of a year it may be able to make a circuit of its entire zone, although sometimes, because of the size of the zone, it is impossible for the Mission to visit a given region more than once in two years. When they return to a district previously visited, the missioners pick up the threads of their previous undertakings and carry on from there, or if the community has fallen below the level at which they left it before, they begin all over again. In any case, there are new problems to face and a great deal that must be done.

Regardless of the varying and trying situations that confront them, it is remarkable how the missioners maintain a spirit of happiness, co-operation, and enthusiasm. There are communities that are antagonistic to the educational programme and particularly to the socialistic ideals of the new education. In such cases the villagers, largely because of a fanatical confidence in the political views and activities of the Church, will take every means to thwart the efforts of the missioners, sometimes going as far as armed opposition and physical violence. One Cultural Mission was stoned out of a village where it had hoped to establish headquarters. Such a small matter did not daunt them. The Mission promptly returned under the leadership of a former army sergeant who replaced a more timid chief. Without resort to force, this Mission was able to carry its programme to a successful completion in that village and, at its close, it left behind a community that was eager for a return engagement! In exceptional cases both the missioners and the rural teachers attending the Institute have found it necessary to wear sidearms and to sleep with a rifle near the bed. Mob violence, arising from religious fanaticism and oftentimes incited by outlawed priests, is one of the things which is taken as a matter of course in the daily work of rural education in Mexico. The benefits of the educational programme are becoming evident to the masses of the people and, slowly but surely, the most rabid opposition to the socialistic programme is giving way to the campaigns by the Cultural Missions and by related agencies.

### Recent Changes in Organization and Practice

Necessarily, the procedures followed by the Cultural Missions have undergone many changes and modifications since they were first started. From time to time their programme has been revised, personnel changes made, and experiments tried in order to determine how to make the work more and more effective.

The most noteworthy of these changes was the attempt, in 1933–1934, to give the work of the Cultural Missions a more lasting character by transforming them from travelling agencies into stationary ones, attached to a rural teacher-training school or an agricultural institution. It was hoped that by this arrangement the Missions would be able to do more in rural rehabilitation and in the cultural enlightenment of peasant and indigenous masses. The process of nationalizing the hitherto neglected masses, with their diversity of languages and with their great variety of economic and social problems, was recognized as being a slow one even at its best. It was hoped that, by locating the Missions permanently in given areas, the campaign of reform would progress at a faster rate since resident cultural agencies could do their work with the people much more thoroughly than was possible on the basis of short intermittent visits. At the same time it was intended that, with a permanent base of operations, the missioners could become better acquainted with the racial, social, and economic requirements of the people and, through their expert knowledge, be in a better position to determine the needs of the rural people and to advise as to the type of federal activity best suited to these needs. Unquestionably, such an arrangement has very much in its favour, and the Cultural Missions were able to accomplish a great deal during the time that they functioned as stationary institutions.

Even though the hopes for such permanent agencies were borne out in every respect, the fact remained that the stationary Missions were reaching only a very small portion of Mexico and that the vast majority of the rural people were being left without the benefit of this valuable cultural influence. The work done in the areas adjacent to the normal and agricultural schools could have justified a continuance of this procedure but, after due deliberation, it was decided that the Missions were of greater value to the nationalizing programme in their character as "*normales ambulantes.*" The choice was between quality and quantity, between regional values and national values. Since a chief function of the Cultural Missions was to break down provincialism and to eliminate cultural contrasts and barriers between regions and classes, there could be but one choice under existing conditions: the Missions had to return to the field.

The advantages accruing to a programme of permanent Cultural Missions, however, are well recognized and attempts are being made to profit by this experiment while, at the same time, the value of the Cultural Missions as travelling agencies is still retained. The rural normal schools and the agricultural schools have modified their programme as well as their methods of procedure so that now they have acquired many of the characteristics of the Cultural Missions. By these modifications, these institutions are able to serve in the capacity of a permanent mission for their respective areas. Indian boarding schools, or *internados,* are constantly carrying on a social-welfare campaign very similar to that of the Missions. Even the regular elementary schools—rural and urban, state and federal —as well as the state secondary schools and colleges are adapting their activities to include some phase of social and community work. This means, then, that the total educational programme in Mexico is assuming the characteristics which, until a year or two ago, were found only in the Cultural Missions and, before them, in the early *misioneros* or supervising teachers.

It would be an exaggeration to say that the Cultural Missions alone are responsible for the great activity that is taking place in this type of work, for this activity is a fundamental principle of the general policy of Mexican government. The great interest that all educational agencies are showing in social and community work reflects the socialist educational philosophy and the revolutionary character of the federal government. It remained for the Cultural Missions, however, to demonstrate this work effectively and to set the example and pattern that other agencies are following with such success.

## An Urban Mission

Knowing of the intensive rural programme and recognizing that the major educational interest of the federal government in Mexico is in the rural areas, it is easy to overlook the valiant efforts that are being made to influence education in the cities. There are many ways in which the Secretariat of Education is attempting to improve urban education and, in a later chapter, we shall examine some of them briefly. An illustration, pertinent to this chapter, is found in the Urban Cultural Mission now operating in the capital cities and in other large centres of population.

Seeking to give city teachers the advantages which the

Cultural Missions have made available to rural teachers, the Secretariat has created a Mission that concerns itself solely with the in-service training of city teachers and with their community (city) problems. At the present time there is only one such agency, though it is likely that more will be created as economic conditions permit. The personnel is made up of a chief of the Mission, who is also professor of national language (Spanish) and arithmetic, a specialist in social sciences, a specialist in natural science, a specialist in physical education, a specialist in music, and one in plastic arts.

The Urban Mission sets up its headquarters in a city and holds a four-week session called the "Institute of Professional Improvement for Teachers." Academic courses are offered by the missioners and considerable work is done in organizing groups and associations (parent-teacher, athletic, and the like). The functions of this Mission are very similar to those of the rural Cultural Missions except that the social and community work in the cities is more limited. During the year 1934–1935 the Urban Cultural Mission visited seven large centres of population in which it held a total of eight Institutes attended by 864 city teachers. These teachers came from both federal and state schools. It is hoped that, by means of these institutions, the work of the city schools can be directed into channels which are proving so successful in rural education. Already one begins to note considerable improvement in the city schools which, not so long ago, were extremely academic and formal in character and whose courses of study were completely unrelated to the practical needs of Mexico.

## Federal Inspectors

The missionary work being done by the federal directors of education in each state and by their corps of inspectors has assumed great importance during the past year or two. Some of the states have turned their schools over to the federal government, thereby placing the responsibility for the entire educational programme in the hands of the Federal Secretariat of Education. The Secretariat, in keeping with its policies and taking advantage of its past experiences, has sought to give the state directors and inspectors considerable prominence in the educational programme. At present there are 30 directors of federal schools. These directors are assisted by an office and supervisory personnel of 139 individuals and by a corps of inspectors or school supervisors. From time to time, both the directors and inspectors are transferred from state to state, often from one end of the country to another. In this way they develop a national attitude in their work and relate the activities of one region to those of others. They are federal field workers, only loosely attached to the administrative processes of a given state. The number of school supervisors was increased from 209 in 1934 to 349 by the latter part of 1935. These inspectors combine the administrative duties of their position with a constant missionary educational campaign in their zones of influence within each state or territory. Each one has charge of not more than 45 schools which he visits periodically, co-ordinating his work with that of other officials, such as Municipal Presidents (Mayors), Labour Inspectors, Agrarian Chiefs, Forest Rangers, etc. He has missionary and supervisory functions that are very similar to those exercised by the Cultural Missions.

The inspectors still retain many of the qualities used to such great advantage by the first missioner-teachers. They see to the selection and placement of teachers, to the construction of buildings and annexes, and to the many problems associated with the activities of a school of action. Travelling alone, or accompanied by an assistant, the inspector is beset with many difficulties. Means of communication are oftentimes lacking. The inspector almost always has to make his circuits on horseback or by canoe, or by relaying between canoe, horseback, and airplane in the flooded regions of Tabasco and Campeche or over the jungles and mountain country of Chiapas. A supervisory trip into the back areas assumes the proportions of a solitary expedition into the wilds of an unknown and unexplored country.

In addition to the handicaps presented by nature there are those presented by rebel gangs known as *"Cristeros,"* "followers of Christ," who, in their religious fanaticism, consider all federal employees and particularly federal school inspectors fair game upon whom to vent the force of their intolerance. I have read numerous anonymous letters written to inspectors in which the recipient was threatened with awesome consequences if he did not refrain from his educational endeavours. Usually these letters are amply illustrated so that there may be no doubt in the inspector's mind as to just what is going to happen to him should he be so foolhardy as to ignore the warning. As a matter of fact, it seldom occurs to the inspector to heed these warnings, though he knows that they are not merely idle threats. He knows that fellow-workers have fallen victims, in verification of these gestures. Regardless of these discouraging aspects, the inspectors and their superior officer, the Director of Education, courageously fulfil the administrative duties of their position and continue to carry on their missionary social service.

The worth of their efforts is mirrored in the success attained by a federal system of rural schools that has grown from 1,000 schools in 1924 to more than 10,000 in 1935—to say nothing of the large number of special schools to which they have contributed much of their time and energy. Under the terms of the "Six-Year Plan," the inspectors and directors must contemplate an increase of 2,000 rural schools in 1936; 2,000 in 1937; 2,000 in 1938; and 3,000 in 1939.

A novel experiment was recently inaugurated by Señor Salvador Varela, until recently Federal Director of Education in the State of Zacatecas and now an Inspector-General for the Secretariat. He equipped a small truck with a gasolene electric generator, motion-picture apparatus, phonograph with radio amplifier, a rural library, and a first-aid kit, and named it the "Travelling Mission for Rural Culture." By means of this truck he was able to make rapid trips into rural areas and to stimulate interest and enthusiasm in the educational programme that he had under way. This Mission serves as a means of attracting the peasants to the school, to a gathering at which plans are being formulated for the building of a school, or to some similar activity. In communities where electric lights are unknown, where there are many people who have never before seen a motion picture or heard music and speeches broadcast through an amplifier, it can readily be seen that this Mission is indeed a great attraction. I have watched the Director and his assistants taking advantage of the novel and magnetic qualities of their equipment to exhort the populace of an isolated hamlet, setting forth their arguments for reform and education. Plans are under way to make this excellent facility available to other states where the condition of the roads warrants its use. The advantages of these motor-missions are readily appreciated; the only obstacle to their widespread use is that the communities most in need of the type of work they offer are the ones that are most isolated and inaccessible. However, with the good roads that exist in some of the states and with the further development of the present intensive road-building programme, a greater use of these agencies is bound to take place.

*The Socialistic Purpose of the Schools*

The complete acceptance of indoctrination is the most striking note in present-day educational thought in Mexico. The schools are not merely educational plants where children and adults learn the fundamentals of literature and mathematics. The schools are organs of propaganda. They are active agents in a plan to change the social and economic order. They do not care to wait for the slow and doubtful reforms which educational evolution might provide. They plunge into the very process of change, modifying and accelerating it in the light of current national ideals and policies. The Mexican schools are schools with a preconceived purpose. They seek to speed up the tempo of community life to the rhythm desired by a central government whose hopes are for an harmonious and progressive national movement. The federal school system, then, is an agency of a revolutionary administration—quite as much so as the Departments of Commerce, War, and the Treasury. Just as one of these departments may seek to reflect the administration's views by constructing a highway through a given region under a specified plan, or by dividing land among the peasants, so the schools attempt to develop the people's ways of thinking and modes of activity along channels which are in keeping with the ideology of the party in power.

The American educator, concerned with the question as to whether the schools should participate in a planned programme or in a planning programme of social and economic development, will find much room for discussion and argument in a study of the Mexican school system. There are both advantages and disadvantages to a campaign of national indoctrination through a centrally controlled school system. A critique of federal policy in Mexico is not within the scope of this interpretative report. It is much more to the point to describe Mexican schools as they are and to try to discover the cause-and-effect relationships between Mexican national growth and the rise of a new system of schools. Any survey of Mexican schools, however, must take into account the fact that the present educational movement is one with national politics —that education and government are inseparable and that schools are agents of a socialistic reform administration.

When one sees that the federal school system is concerned with bringing about a rapid change from the old colonial order to a new socialistic order, the value of the educational missionary agencies assumes greater proportions. If Mexico had to await the slow and tedious process of education of children only and of a standard programme of teacher-training, with the resultant delay in popular enlightenment and community development, the reforms of the revolution would be delayed for at least one or two generations. Even then it would have to be assumed that Mexico had the facilities to carry on an adequate teacher-training programme and that her teachers would be capable of transplanting into the remote and backward villages the knowledge acquired in normal schools and teachers' colleges. It would have to be taken for granted that Mexican teachers would be competent in adapting their knowledge to the varying and contrasting situations which would confront them in the wide expanse of Mexican territory and among the dissimilar groups that constitute the Mexican people. It goes without saying that such a situation would be fraught with grave dangers as well as intolerable delays.

The plan of action of the federal government, wherein the administration projects itself and its policies directly into the schools and into the villages, is quite in keeping with a revolutionary programme. It exhibits the governmental concern that is felt for the welfare of the nation and indicates a complete acceptance of the will of the people as learned from the popular demonstrations of the past—particularly from the proletarian Revolution of 1910–1920. The front-line place given to the educational missions in this plan of action adds to the importance of these institutions, both in their scholastic functions and in their role as agencies of a political New Deal.

The Cultural Missions serve not only as teacher-training and social-welfare agencies but in the much more important capacity of bridging the gap between theory and practice. The Cultural Missions, and the other agencies that exercise similar missionary functions, represent both the most advanced thinking in Mexico and the actual application of social and educational theories *in situ*. Their primary function is that of "incorporation." They must integrate the Mexican peoples and Mexican practices into a national fold and into a co-ordinated progressive trend. The Cultural Missions stand for what is new in education, in agrarian reforms, in economic practices, in political policies, and in social relationships. Born of dire need, they represent all the elements that distinguish modern Mexico from old Mexico. They symbolize the change from feudalism to socialism, from exploitation to co-operation, from slavery to freedom. They wage a revolution by education.

# CHAPTER VI

# THE SOCIALISTIC SCHOOL

THE rise of a socialistic school programme in Mexico represents a stage of development in the unfolding of a national consciousness among her peoples. Socialistic schools are simply the latest expression of a growing tide of liberalism that began in colonial days.

It would be easy to think of the change from the old type of schools to popular education as being sudden—accomplished solely by the stroke of a successful revolution. It is more correct to interpret the Socialistic School in terms of a long period of slow growth and to recognize that the new educational movement in Mexico is merely the blossoming of tendencies that have been in the process of growth for centuries. The early colonial schools were radical departures from anything that existed in Europe and were, in a sense, the first steps taken by New Spain in achieving individuality. These schools recognized those problems that were peculiar to Mexico and adapted their programmes to meet the unique situations of the new environment and occasioned by the enrolment of Indians, *mestizos*, and Spanish-Mexicans. The schools of the nineteenth century, by seeking to eliminate the religious aspects from their programme and by stressing freedom of thought, symbolized the rise of a liberal group and began to assume the marks of state schools with a state function. The rudimentary schools established during the first twenty years of the present century were indications of the attempt to bring the masses of the Mexican people into the Mexican cultural fold. These schools failed in their purpose largely because their programme had little relationship to Mexican life as it was. The general picture of educational development in Mexico is clouded and distorted by the educational imperfections through which a Mexican cultural consciousness was sought. The fact remains, however, that there has been a very definite and long-continued tendency toward the incorporation of the Mexican people into a cultural unity.

The names by which the schools have been known since 1920 are illustrative of the evolution of schools with a distinctly social point of view. First of all there was "The House of the People," essentially a governmental attempt to solidify and socialize Mexican villages through a cultural institution. A little later we saw the rise of "The Schools of Action," in which the academic and social functions of the school are given a more dynamic aspect. These schools stressed the importance of objective instruction and of active co-operation between the various divisions of social and economic life in rural communities. They were primarily concerned with stimulating the constructive phases of community growth. Following these schools of action came "The School of Work," which dedicated itself to education through manual activities rather than through study that was purely academic and intellectual. It was believed that the work-project type of instruction should be the fundamental activity of schools that had by this time become well entrenched as popular institutions. Each new aim has developed out of the preceding one and, through a natural growth of the schools and of educational theory, each new principle has been superimposed on the previous one to form a unified system of ideals grounded on popular welfare.

This general development of educational theory was not unrelated to the political growth of Mexico but formed a part of the total progressive trend. The names by which the schools were known at various stages between 1920 and 1935 could just as well be applied to the steps taken by the Mexican nation in political and economic fields from 1810 until the present time. Beginning with the "rudimentary" *criollo* governments shortly after Independence, through the popular tendencies of the reform movement around 1857, through the materialistic reconstruction of the Díaz period, and on to the proletarian socialism of the Revolution and of the revolutionary governments, national growth seems to have pointed out the trend for educational growth. This is particularly true of the governments of the peaceful revolution. Mexican government between 1920 and 1925 distinguished itself as a popular government, of and for the people. Succeeding years saw much national activity and construction. The work-project idea in federal administration was added to a form of governmental control that was basically popular and democratic and was a long way from political rule achieved through shady manipulations and military *coups*. The Mexican school programme reflects and is a part of every step taken in national growth and can be understood only in terms of Mexico's emergence from provincialism to nationalism.

The socialist point of view of Mexican government is best illustrated by describing the administration of national affairs in Mexico as government through social intervention, or government through extensive, federally directed, popular education. In view of the nationalistic tendencies of Mexican development, it devolved upon the central government to assume those activities which were most definitely related to the growth of Mexico as a nation. As agencies of the State, the schools form the front rank in the campaign of national renovation and reconstruction. The important part assigned to education in this growth has made it imperative that the central government assume direct responsibility for the control and direction of schools and of educational thought.

In 1920 the federal government controlled education only in the Federal District (corresponding to the District of Columbia) and in the territories (Lower California and Quintana Roo at the southern end of the Yucatán peninsula). By reforms inaugurated in 1922, the federal government was authorized to enter the educational field in the various states. This participation was at first limited to the inauguration of a programme of rural schools that would supplement the work of the schools maintained and controlled by the states. The federal system of rural schools gradually expanded and developed the type of programme which is suggested in the description of the Cultural Missions in the preceding chapter. This network of schools formed the fountain from which flowed the new idealism and the system acted as the voice of the revolutionary government in its quest for socioeconomic reforms.

The success which met the efforts of the rural schools and the effective manner in which these rural schools were able to meet the needs of the people suggested that their influence be extended. This led to the introduction of the rural type of education into the urban centres and of the general modification of the theory and practice of city schools. A programme which was created to give a minimum education in the fundamentals to the underprivileged rural masses took the educational limelight and proceeded to enter the field of urban education. The rural "elementary-primary" school (grades 1, 2, 3, and 4) was considered inadequate, and the "superior-primary" grades (5 and 6) are rapidly being added to all rural schools in order that the *campesino* may have the advantage of a complete course in elementary education. In its march into the field of city schools, the federal government has not been content to limit its influence to primary instruction but has undertaken to set the pace in secondary (grades 7, 8, and 9), technical, and industrial education. Gradually the national schools—rural and urban, primary and secondary, vocational and technical, for children and adults—are co-ordinating Mexican life and taking dominant place in the national incorporation and redemption.

The federal government has exercised its educational functions so successfully that some of the states, in spite of a general unwillingness to relinquish states' rights, have placed their schools entirely under the direction of the central authority. During 1935 five states signed pacts with the central government by which they consented to place their state-supported schools in the hands of the Secretariat of Education and by which they agreed to continue giving financial assistance to those schools. The schools in four other states were being administered by the Secretariat even though no compact had been formally signed. Other states will enter into this arrangement gradually, and it appears that within a few years education in Mexico will become completely federalized.

The strides taken by the national government in introducing the new type of federal school into all parts of Mexico and in seeking to assume control of the total educational programme of the country speaks for the importance placed on education as a governmental instrument for achieving the nationalism that Mexico has heretofore lacked. This centralizing tendency is, in effect, a recognition of the principle that the new education is a product of the Revolution; that the proletariat, by right of popular conquest, is entitled to cultural enlightenment; and that the federal administration is the voice of the victorious revolutionaries and, therefore, the proper agency in which to vest the responsibility for waging a nationalistic cultural revolution. For better or for worse, the revolutionary generation has placed its trust in a federal socialistic school—an institution bred on Mexican soil, born of popular faith and hope, and nourished on the zealous devotion and love that is Mexican patriotism. Federal activity, in founding schools for the people, is not an artificial gesture nor merely a political trump card. It bespeaks attentiveness to the voice of the people —to the wishes of the masses.

### The Socialistic School Programme

The first social problem of the new schools was to entrench themselves as community centres in rural areas. That is to say, the schools first sought to become community-centred organizations as contrasted with child-centred schools or institutions whose activities revolved around traditional subject matter. Having achieved this through "The House of the People," "The School of Action," "The School of Work," and through the aggressive activity of the *misioneros* and Cultural Missions, the federal government was ready to take the next step in its educational plan. Within the past two years schools have been given an additional function, represented by the name by which the federal school is now known, "The Socialistic School." The schools are no longer to be satisfied with an intensive campaign to raise the social and economic level of the communities in which they operate; they are to become active forces in moulding public opinion towards a better understanding and an acceptance of the ideals of socialistic government. Still seriously concerned with the economic problems of the masses—with health and sanitation, with literacy, with arts and crafts—they have been vested with an additional responsibility as socialistic organs.

## CONSTITUTIONAL BASES OF MEXICAN EDUCATION

### ARTICLE 3 OF THE CONSTITUTION OF THE UNITED MEXICAN STATES

Article 3—The education imparted by the State shall be a socialistic one and, in addition to excluding all religious doctrine, shall combat fanaticism and prejudices by organizing its instruction and activities in a way that shall permit the creation in youth of an exact and rational concept of the Universe and of social life.

Only the State—Federation, States, Municipalities—shall impart primary, secondary, and normal education. Authorization may be conceded to individuals who desire to impart education in any of the aforementioned three levels in conformity, in every case, with the following norms:

I. The teachings and activities of private plants must adjust themselves without exception to that indicated in the initial paragraph of this Article and shall be in charge of persons who, in the opinion of the State, shall have sufficient professional preparation and a morality and ideology that is suitable to and in keeping with this precept. In view of this, religious corporations, the ministers of cults, the organizations which preferably or exclusively carry on educational activities, and the associations or societies bound directly or indirectly to the propaganda of a religious creed shall in no way intervene in primary, secondary, or normal schools, nor shall they be permitted to assist these financially.

II. The formation of plans, programmes, and methods of teaching shall in every case rest in the State.

III. Private plants shall not be permitted to function without first, and in each case, having obtained the express authorization of the public power.

IV. The State may at any time revoke the authorization granted (to private individuals or organizations). There shall be no judgment or recourse whatsoever against such revocation.

The same norms shall govern the education of whatever type or grade that is imparted to workers or peasants.

Primary education shall be obligatory, and the State shall impart it gratuitously.

The State may, at its discretion and at any time, withdraw recognition of official validity to the studies made in private plants.

The Congress of the Union, in the interest of unifying and coordinating education throughout the Republic, shall promulgate the necessary laws destined to distribute the social educative function between the Federation and the States and Municipalities, to fix the financial apportionments corresponding to that public service, and to indicate the sanctions (penalties) applicable to those functionaries who do not comply with, or force compliance to, the respective dispositions, as well as to all those who violate them.

The Mexican schools of today are described and guided by the following five principles:

1. The Socialistic School is Revolutionary. It seeks to accelerate the process of cultural, social, and economic development among the people. It is not satisfied to await the results of an evolutionary process by which, in time, the people might reap the fruits of a standard type of education. Pressed by the urgency of the situation, these schools are striving to bridge the gap of time by becoming active agents in the process of social change.

2. The Socialistic School is Proletarian. Its chief interest lies in the masses of the people and in the unification, or nationalization, of these masses for their benefit and in their interests. The new schools are proletarian as contrasted with the bourgeois schools that had existed in Mexico before 1920. They are concerned with the problems of the middle and upper classes only to the extent that such an interest may be of benefit to the great masses of the Mexican people. In a sense they may be described as being anti-bourgeois, anti-aristocratic, and anti-capitalistic. Through every phase of their programme of activities, they seek to carry on a programme of socialization and of nationalization.

3. The Socialistic School is a Nationalistic School—a school that believes in the creation of a national spirit and that is militant in behalf of the cultural and economic sovereignty of Mexico as a nation. It is a school that wants Mexico for Mexicans and that seeks to stimulate an appreciation of the value of Mexican ideas, Mexican institutions, Mexican accomplishments, and Mexican culture. It seeks to accentuate those aspects of Mexican life that give Mexico individuality and character as a nation. In short, it insists that Mexico is no longer a colonial province to be exploited at will by foreign nations and ideas but rather that Mexico is a sovereign power with cultural attributes worthy of recognition.

4. The Socialistic School is a Popular School—democratic as contrasted to aristocratic. It seeks to exercise a levelling influence whereby the masses of the people are raised to a position of the greatest prominence in Mexican life. It is eager to train the proletariat in such a way that the whole of Mexican life shall reflect the will of the great majority of the people. This democratic ideal, carried to the point of socialism, is the essence of the things for which Mexicans have hoped and which has been back of Mexican rebellions against domination and exploitation.

5. The Socialistic School is Rationalistic, endeavouring to inculcate beliefs that stand the test of intellectual and rational examination. Many of the evils by which Mexico and Mexicans have been beset are generally attributed to the docility of the Mexican masses in blindly accepting the point of view of exploiting agencies. One purpose of the Socialistic School is to counteract the docile acceptance of religious beliefs and superstitions by introducing a rationalizing element into the thinking of the people. While the School is not interested in combating the spiritual beliefs inculcated by religion, it is extremely interested in seeing that an unthinking acceptance or extension of these beliefs does not interfere with the social, economic, and cultural well-being of Mexicans. It makes every effort to divorce the spiritual life of the individual from his daily social and civic practices. Particularly, it seeks to emphasize in the minds of the masses the difference between religion, as a purely personal and spiritual belief, and the political and economic

practices of religious organizations. It desires to free the devout and fanatical masses from the cultural and economic exploitation carried on by the corporate bodies who represent the agencies for the dissemination of religious beliefs.

These five tenets of the school are, it is true, the expressed desire rather than an accomplished fact. As Frank Tannenbaum has said in *Peace by Revolution:*

This program of ideas and ideals came to the fore more or less consciously, more or less rapidly, as the project of building schools, finding teachers, developing a school organization, began to be undertaken seriously. The ideal was clear enough. I remember Vasconcelos once saying to me, "We have all the ideas we need, more than we can use. What we need is money, resources, people, details, persistence." The ideas have grown with the years. So has the inventiveness, so have the concrete projects and plans, and so, one might add, have the people. But the ideal and real were far apart. It was no easy task to give Mexico an educational system, no easy task to undertake to do in a few years what had been neglected for four centuries. Not even the enthusiasm of the Revolution and the missionary zeal it left in its wake have been sufficient to consummate that task—and it remains an ideal, the fulfilment of which will require more than one generation of self-sacrifice and enthusiasm and faith.

## The Present Schools

On January 1, 1935, President Lázaro Cárdenas devoted considerable space in his presidential message to the educational undertaking of the government. At that time he stated: "We believe that the Mexican Revolution has arrived at a stage of social maturity and that it is possible to encompass [in the educational programme] the integral aspect of national problems . . . the Socialistic School shall convert itself into a focus of sane social activity which identifies the life of the community with the school itself, forming a homogeneous whole. . . ." This point of view expresses the essence of what the new school is supposed to be. The school is not simply concerned with *preparing* for life activities. Rather, the school is life itself and forms an active part of the total social structure. The Secretary of Education, commenting on the President's address, added: "Education shall be directed with preference towards the peasant and working classes and shall be based on the problems of the environment." The pupils of the new school, then, are the Mexican masses and the curriculum is based on the life problems of the Mexican peoples.

These ideals have been expressed many times before by those who would co-ordinate the life of the school with the life of the community in which the school operates. In the United States we have proposed this doctrine often but, except in rare instances, have not achieved the success desired. The attempt to apply these theories in Mexico does not always result in the integration of school and community life. Yet there are many schools where one may observe the operation of these principles and where beginnings at least have been made in carrying out these ideas. In a mining town in Chihuahua I have observed a federal school that was functioning as the commissary and base of operations for the miners who, at the time, were engaged in a strike. The school teacher, the inspector of the zone, and the children themselves played active roles in supporting the striking miners in their struggle for better wages and better working conditions. The Chief of Police of the City of Chihuahua, with the aid of his officers and some of the prisoners, had constructed a small school building in a poor and isolated section of the city. This school, "José Dolores Palomino," was neat, well-equipped, and was looked upon with justifiable pride by the police force and by the residents of the district. It not only set an example for the people of the city but it served as a bond of co-operation and mutual understanding between the law-enforcing body and that section of the community wherein much of the crime of the city was bred.

Visits to many schools in almost every part of the Republic confirm the opinion that the new schools of Mexico are really striving to meet their responsibilities as community schools and as socializing centres. The school on the Island of Janitzio in Lake Pátzcuaro, State of Michoacán, is vastly different from schools in other parts of the state and other parts of the nation. Yet it embodies the same principles under which all schools operate and adapts them to its peculiar situation. The children and adults are taught the intricacies of the art of making useful articles, decorated with beautiful lacquer work. They learn to perform their native Tarascan dances to traditional Tarascan songs and music. With land unsuitable for farming, the Indians of this region have earned a meagre living by seining fish in Lake Pátzcuaro. The schools have undertaken to improve their condition by training them in arts and crafts so that they may supplement their earnings as fishermen.

Federal schools in the alluvial plains of south-eastern Mexico are similarly occupied, but in an environment different from that observed for the region of Lake Pátzcuaro. Oftentimes the children have to go to and from school in canoes. The schoolroom is nothing more than a ramshackle thatched hut, situated on rising ground which, during the rainy season, is an island in a turbulent sea of flood waters. Classes are often held in a cloud cf smoke from smudge pots which must be kept burning to drive away the swarms of mosquitoes, horseflies, spiders, ticks, and other insects. Ordinarily one-third of the children enrolled are out of school because of malarial chills and fever or because of other illnesses which are aggravated by their undernourished condition. Children are taught the cultivation of vegetables and fruits and the schoolground forms the garden where agricultural practices are carried on. Because of the difficulties of communication and owing to the dangers from snakes, particularly the *nahuyacas*, vicious and deadly vipers that frequent footpaths in the evening, it is impossible to hold night classes for adults. This makes it necessary for the rural teacher to try to bring the grown-up members of the community to the school during the daytime. This he does by enlisting their co-operation in the repair of the schoolhouse, in the clearing of a plot of ground for the garden, in planting, and in similar activities. Incidentally, the school teacher points out the advantages of a balanced diet to supplant or supplement the *posole* to which they are accustomed and which often forms the only food at their disposal.

It is inevitable that schools founded on revolutionary principles should be subject to various interpretations and varying applications. Over-zealous directors, inspectors, and teachers may at times give undue emphasis to one or another of the new theories and thus arouse criticism and resentment. It is easy to see how these principles might be misconstrued in practice to such a point that federal education could be charged with extreme radicalism or even with communism—elements which, in reality, are counter to the general programme of federal education. What is true of these principles of education is true of the total programme of the revolutionary government and, quite often, undue attention is attracted to a miscarriage of the ideals involved.

During the summer of 1935, for example, the attention of the world was focused on the activities inspired by the resignation from President Cárdenas's cabinet of Señor Tomás Garrido Canabal—an ultra-radical exponent of an extreme interpretation of the federal policy. Garrido Canabal's followers, the so-called "Red Shirts," had incited armed and destructive demonstrations against legal and orderly religious practices and against institutions, organizations, and even buildings that were directly or indirectly connected with the Church. In addition to their participation in licentiousness, destruction, and even in massacres, their activities did much to discredit the efforts of the government for an orderly and peaceful revolution.

During the height of Garrido Canabal's power, attendance at town meetings in the State of Tabasco was compulsory. School pupils were organized into young "Red Shirts" and were induced to wear this special garb as a symbol of their radicalism. Participation in public festivals was an obligation rather than a privilege. In sum, socialism was enforced by imposition and dictation. When, with Garrido Canabal's fall from grace, a group of students left Mexico City to campaign in Tabasco for a saner and more conservative application of socialism, they became involved in a pitched battle with the radical element on the streets of Villahermosa, the capital city. The loss of life in this encounter focused attention on the dangers of an extreme interpretation of Mexico's programme. Other demonstrations in other parts of the country have had similar results and have tended to bring about the acceptance of a more orderly process in the unfolding of the socialistic ideals.

The practices of these ultra-enthusiasts must not be condemned in their entirety. Though their efforts to speed up the process of incorporation may be misguided and over-ambitious, yet side by side with their excesses they have established monuments that do credit to the new ideals. While the State of Tabasco has abolished churches, it has also curtailed the demoralizing use of alcoholic beverages. Even in this reform it has gone to the excess of "prohibition" rather than temperance. At Villahermosa I was impressed with the fine wards in which houses for the workers had been constructed by the government or through the co-operative efforts of the labour organizations and city and state officials. The consolidated open-air schools, "Alvaro Obregón" and "Plutarco Elías Calles," on the outskirts of Villahermosa, do credit to the humanitarian ideals of their founder, Garrido Canabal.

These schools, built on the high ground away from the unhealthy low-lying central part of the city, are fascinating projects. Attendance is compulsory and transportation to and from the schools is free, as are also well-balanced noonday lunches. Each of the schools assumes the proportions of a communistic agricultural village. Extensive fields are planted and cultivated by the students and the proceeds distributed among the student body. Various forms of co-operative activity are carried on and school government is largely in the hands of the pupils. Parent-teacher organizations participate in the programme and assist in the construction and repair of the thatched schoolrooms which are strung out in a series about the farm-school ground. While formal classes in the fundamentals are a part of school life, a great portion of the day is devoted to the work of managing and operating the school farm. The children attend to the cattle, the chickens, and the other animals. They plant their co-operative plots, take care of various fruit trees, and carry on a very real community life. Each classroom consists of nothing more than a thatched roof supported by poles. Classroom equipment is limited to school desks, a blackboard, and a few textbooks and supplementary readers. The situation of the school and the work carried on by the students are conducive to both physical and mental well-being. It is clear that this arrangement is much better than the one previously followed, wherein the children were cooped in dark and poorly ventilated school buildings situated in the damp, low-lying environs of Villahermosa proper.

Regardless of the handicaps imposed by inadequate or mis-guided administration and in spite of the obstacles presented by the environment, the federal rural schools attempt to practise the principles preached in the socialist doctrine of the central government. Modifying their procedures to meet the peculiarities of each individual situation, these schools, never-theless, are all guided by the same principles. In this respect they present a united front in the campaign of nationalization.

## Urban and Part-Time Schools

The Socialistic School is fundamentally a rural school for, in the words of President Cárdenas in his Message for 1935, "As the rural population exceeds 66 per cent of the inhabitants; as this population is far removed from the sources of education; given the nature of their work activities and the hygienic, domestic, and social conditions in which they live; because of their lack of resources and owing to their particular ideology, *the task of national education demands the diffusion of learn-ing in the rural areas* as one of its principal obligations." How-ever, the fundamental mission of the federal school is that of "incorporation"—of integrating all of the diverse conditions in Mexico into a progressive and unified national order. This means that the Socialistic School cannot be limited to those areas that are definitely rural in character. It must go wherever there is need for rehabilitation and incorporation. It can be seen that the action of the Socialistic School must be extended from rural fields into urban centres. This is being done with some degree of success through various agencies. The Rural Department of the Secretariat of Education has established 16 "Model" primary schools in capital cities, 371 "Semi-Urban" primary schools in the principal cities of the political subdivisions of the states, and 58 kindergartens, making a total of 445 "rural" schools in the field of town and city education. These schools were under the direction of 1,113 federal teachers. In addition to these strictly federal schools, the Secretariat controlled a total of 163 primary state-supported schools in the cities as well as 188 state-supported rural schools. All of these are in addition to the regular rural schools and in addition to secondary schools and colleges.

The "Model" schools, operating in the capitals, are endeavouring to introduce into the urban centres the community activities which characterize the operation of rural schools. During the day they hold classes for the children while at night they devote themselves to the instruction of adults. Adult education consists of instruction in reading, writing, accounting, sewing, cooking, etc. These schools inaugurate campaigns that meet their socializing function; they direct every effort towards the reduction of alcoholism and illiteracy; and they act in the interest of health and sanitation. Each school functions on a one-year plan or programme in which the procedures and aims of the work to be accomplished in that year are set forth. Each year this plan is revised and renewed.

The "Semi-Urban" schools are more closely related to the rural type of education owing to the fact that they operate in smaller centres of population. In addition to carrying on their activities with the children and the adults of the town in which they are located, these schools serve as model centres for the rural teachers in the region surrounding the town. Most of these schools have agricultural grounds and the various *anexos:* open-air theatres, playgrounds and athletic courts, pig sties, chicken coops, libraries, etc. These *anexos* serve as working models for the community as a whole, for the children, and for the teachers of the area. They form an integral part of the curriculum and represent the type of activity that many of the rural schools are engaged in and with which they are achieving so much success. It is a poor rural school, indeed, that does not have a garden plot, a pigeon house, rabbit hutches, and an improved playground. Many of them go far beyond these minimum essentials. A village park, a community flower garden, a decorative fountain for the plaza, and even a village market-place may be an *anexo* to a humble one-room rural school.

The fifty-eight kindergartens operated by the Secretariat have undertaken to introduce children of pre-school age to the Socialistic School. These kindergartens are usually conducted as annexes to semi-urban or model schools. Songs and dances, gardening, miniature constructions, and plays and games, as well as the ever-present swimming pool, are utilized in smoothing the path between home and school. The average Mexican kindergarten is superior to the general run of kindergartens found in the United States, for it represents real-life activities of children in an educational setting much more successfully than I have observed in the American institution.

The Secretariat has been experimenting with a type of part-time school particularly charged with the education of adults. By October 1935, there were six "Cultural Centres for Workers" located in four different states. During the day or in the evening workers may, at their convenience, receive instruction at these centres. The schedule of these schools is flexible and is adjusted to the social and economic environment and to the needs of the adults of the area. The part-time school seeks to reduce illiteracy and give general instruction in domestic science, in hygiene and sanitation, and in those fields that are specifically related to the needs of the given town or city.

Part of the time in these schools is given to civic education and to cultural and social activities such as the organization of literary, music, and athletic clubs. Some industries have minimum educational standards for their workers, and it is a function of the cultural centres to prepare workers to meet these requirements. In addition to their work in adult education these institutions often supplement the efforts of the regular schools. It is not unusual to find adults and children working together on some project of mutual interest and benefit at a Workers' Cultural Centre. While the difference between the adults' and children's classes is well recognized, joint classes, with adults and children as pupils, are often the result of some natural situation. In one instance I observed a primary class in second-grade reading where the soldiers from the local garrison were voluntarily and painstakingly participating as students along with the youngsters, some of whom were the children of the soldier-pupils. From all appearances the classes were quite successful and did not occasion any embarrassment or difficulties to the children, the soldiers, or the youthful teacher. The soldiers considered it a great privilege to be able to attend a school in their leisure moments and were a fine influence as pupils. Instances such as this illustrate the general acceptance of a national educational campaign and the great desire that the Mexican people have for the rudiments of knowledge. There are, with few exceptions, as many night schools for adults as there are federal schools, whether these be rural or urban, primary or secondary, large or small.

### Private and State Schools

In keeping with the provisions of Article 3 of the Constitution, all private schools engaged in elementary, secondary, or normal school instruction must conform to the regulations of the federal government or close their doors. As those schools which were directly or indirectly connected with a religious organization are expressly forbidden by the Constitution, hundreds of these schools were closed with the publication of the new provisions. However, many private schools have continued to operate by securing proper authorization from federal authorities. By the middle of 1935, 114 private elementary schools had received such authorization. The federal school inspectors visit these private institutions, supervise their courses and programme of work, determine whether or not the teaching personnel is qualified in both professional preparation and social ideology, investigate the adequacy of the school buildings and materials, and pass on whether or not the institutions meet the federal requirements.

There are several instances where private schools are carrying on valuable education. The American School in Mexico City and a large private school situated at Mazatlán fill a real need. As a general rule, however, existing private schools are extremely formal and are unrelated to the active programme of education being carried on by the federal school system. Ordinarily they are conducted for financial gain and are but little concerned with the socializing function that is such an important part of the Mexican plan. The patrons of these schools are those who still feel an attachment for the old type of formal academic instruction, those who rebel against sending their children to the Socialistic School, or those who are unable to find a place for their children in the overcrowded federal schools. In view of the many restrictions on private education, and in view of the rapid growth of public schools, it is conceivable that in a short time private schools will disappear completely, except in a few cases where they fill a specific function not met by the general school system.

State-supported schools, particularly those that have been federalized (that is, placed under control and administration of the national Secretariat of Education), are gradually conforming to the aims and procedures of the federal system. The federal directors of education, as well as the inspectors, make every effort to assist state schools in modernizing their curricula and in introducing methods whereby the schools may be related to the needs of the community. Through joint teachers' meetings, through Institutes conducted by federal authorities, through an exchange of teachers between city and rural schools, and through the supervisory and co-operative efforts of the Missions and the school inspectors, state schools are constantly being brought into contact with the new procedures and fresh ideals of their more progressive and more active federal counterparts. As the federal "model" and "semi-urban" schools and kindergartens exist side by side with state-supported institutions, these federal agencies serve as models for the state schools and act in a missionary capacity in modernizing state schools. The states are rapidly withdrawing from the field of rural education—a field that, with few exceptions, has been taken over by the Rural Department of the Secretariat of Education. Slowly but surely, directly or indirectly, the federal office is also taking over the guidance and the control of the city schools.

It is generally conceded that federal schools, whether urban or rural, are superior to schools maintained and administered by the states or by municipalities. The advantages are to be found not only in the programme of studies of the schools but also in the amount of supervision offered, in the general benefits to the community, and in the higher professional status of the federal teachers. The Secretariat has a well-defined and legalized plan of tenure and promotion for the federal teachers who also participate in the federal pension and retirement system and whose salaries are governed by a standardized schedule. When state schools become federalized, they automatically become entitled to many of these advantages, although the regulations pertaining to salary schedules, pensions, tenure, and promotion apply only in so far as the state is willing and able to accept the financial requirements of these guarantees. Federal schools have met with such great success, and federalized state schools have shown so much improvement over their previous status, that it appears reasonable to assume that within a period of a few years all the schools in Mexico will function either as federal schools or as federalized state and municipal schools. Even private schools are so closely regulated and supervised by federal provisions and authorities that these may soon be looked upon as a part of the federal system.

## The Teachers

The most impressive aspect of the entire new educational movement in Mexico is the part played by the Mexican school teacher. It is puzzling to understand how it has been possible for a group of teachers, selected more or less at random, to fit so well into the new movement. These teachers, to begin with, were not academically trained. They had little or no professional preparation, no experience, and they had obtained their positions because the Secretariat had launched a school project and had to have individuals to direct the schools regardless of the fact that suitably trained teachers were not available. Since they began their teaching careers, these people have been assisted by the Cultural Missions, the inspectors, and occasionally by courses offered in normal schools. This training has been of great value in assisting the teacher to recognize and attack the educational responsibilities presented at the scene of his labours.

The assistance and guidance given by governmental institutions cannot alone explain the devotion and enthusiasm with which the Mexican teacher dedicates his life to the cultural revolution. This interest in educational work is not limited to women. It is surprising to note that teaching positions are about evenly distributed between the sexes. It is even more surprising to find that men comprise more than two-thirds of the enrolment in normal schools. It cannot be said that the teacher's salary is much of an inducement. A daily wage of 60 cents, from which are deducted the percentages for the retirement plan and for various dues, does not present an irresistible attraction. This is especially true when one considers the conditions under which the teachers live and work in remote villages and the arduous nature of their teaching tasks. Ordinarily the regular day school is conducted between nine in the morning and five in the afternoon, with a noonday intermission. As a general rule, each school, no matter how remote or how small, conducts adult-education classes between six and ten in the evening. Community activities, teachers' institutes, and participation in the social and civic life of the region place additional responsibilities and duties on the teachers. In the face of such a heavy programme, and though the yearly turnover in teachers is approximately 40 per cent, recruits are always available from the ranks of normal-school graduates and, as these are not nearly enough, from among the ranks of the general population.

It would be justifiable to predict that under these conditions the teaching personnel would be incapable of doing justice to the aims of federal socialist education. Yet direct observation of many of these schools in action and a critical evaluation of their educational and social achievements demonstrate that such a prediction is erroneous. It would seem that the very lack of preparation and the very difficulty of the task which they have willingly assumed make it possible for Mexican teachers to introduce the socializing educational function of the Mexican schools much more ably than could more sophisticated individuals who were academically prepared to handle school problems in a more professional manner. It is, of course, preposterous to suggest that insufficient preparation of the personnel is responsible for the success of the Mexican rural school. It must be assumed that a process of selection is operating whereby those individuals who are by temperament and attitude best suited to a revolutionary programme are the ones who seek and remain in teaching positions. It must also be assumed that, to the degree that the federal government makes additional training and guidance available to these teachers, the future accomplishments of the schools will be increased in value and in scope.

The broad range of the tasks assigned to Mexican teachers and the financial and physical obstacles to the successful operation of the schools are not the only handicaps. The hostility evidenced towards the socialist aims of the Administration by portions of the Mexican people places many a teacher in the position of having to withstand the opposition of his or her patrons and of converting them to the new ideals. This process of conversion is frequently very dangerous to the teacher and may be illustrated by the simple and almost casual statement of the Department of Rural Education: *"Fifteen rural teachers have fallen victims to religious and capitalistic reaction."* The Secretariat of Education, through this parenthetical observation, takes passing notice of the murder of rural teachers by fanatical outlaws who seek to thwart the type of education prescribed by the Mexican Constitution. In a recent demonstration by teachers in Mexico City an immense parade was led by two rural school teachers who had literally "given their ears" to the cause of rural education! The activities of *Cristeros* and similar groups do not seriously dampen the ardour of the Mexican teachers, for that is accepted as part of the task which they voluntarily shoulder. Recently I asked a director if religious fanatics had given much trouble in a particular zone of his state. In a somewhat offhand manner he replied, "Not a great deal; we have lost only three teachers in eight months."

Just as the federal government has tried to strengthen the professional training of its teachers, it has also tried to give them some degree of security in the daily exercise of their duties. During the latter part of 1935 the Ministry of War issued final instructions to the heads of military zones to the effect that federal teachers must be given immediate and effective protection. At the same time it has made it legally possible for school teachers to carry arms and to take such steps as may be necessary to safeguard their lives from rebellious elements. Trials and tribulations of this nature are part of the day's work for the rural teachers.

Unlike the directors and inspectors who are transferred from zone to zone and from state to state periodically and at the discretion of the federal office, the teachers are sent to communities with which they are thoroughly familiar, quite often the ones where they were born and raised. Because of this, the teacher is closer to the people of the community and is in an advantageous position in judging the problems and needs of the people. The teacher becomes a leader in the village and, through his rise to such a position of leadership, he serves as a living example to his relatives and friends, justifying the parents' hope for a brighter future for their children. The official position which the teacher holds, the active part that he plays in federal activities in the region, and his close relationship with agrarian organizations, land banks, and other governmentally stimulated agencies give him additional prestige and prominence. By official and personal leadership and by fitting into current village practices he is in a position to bring about gradual improvements and to introduce new ideas with the least possible friction and shock. This is assuming, of course, that the teacher possesses a high degree of tact and common sense; strange as it may seem, these are qualifications which are almost second nature to the Mexican rural teacher. The constant supervision exercised by the director and his inspectors and by the Cultural Missions bolsters the individual accomplishments of the teacher and serves to guide him into the paths which are of greatest promise in terms of his capacities and in view of the problems which he has to meet.

## The Department of Rural Education

The Department of Rural Education of the Secretariat has borne the major portion of the responsibility for establishing a national system of schools. Previous to 1934, various departments and bureaux were charged with the administration of the several types of schools. In 1934 the federal system of education began to operate under a well-defined schedule set up by the national administrative plan of work known as the Six-Year Plan, and more definite direction was given to the activities of the Secretariat. In that same year (1934) the Department of Rural Education of the Secretariat was formed from existing departments and bureaux and was given control of all the elementary schools managed by the federal government, with the exception of the schools in the Federal District.

In view of the responsibilities placed on the Department of Rural Education by the requirements of the Six-Year Plan, it was necessary that a technical and advisory planning council be set up in that department to direct and co-ordinate the educational programme. A *"Cuerpo Técnico de Educación Rural"* was established and five leading educators, including Professor Rafael Ramírez and Señorita Elena Torres, were named as the technical experts. From the time of its creation, this board has served as the guiding element in federal education. It concerns itself with the formulation of courses of study and methods of procedure as well as with questions which arise in regard to the expansion of the federal school system. In effect, it serves as the "brain trust" for the Rural Department and as a valuable advisory body for the entire Secretariat. It co-operates with all departments of the Ministry of Education and is probably the agency most representative of the careful study and preparation that are being given to the educational needs of Mexico and to the formulation of plans for the progress of the cultural revolution.

The Department of Rural Education controls rural elementary education, kindergartens, primary model schools, semi-urban primary schools, workers' cultural centres, Indian schools, and federalized state primary schools. This represents practically the whole of Mexican schools. Besides these, there are only the rural normal and agricultural schools which are administered by the department of that name (which also has control of Cultural Missions); the technical and industrial schools, also administered by a separate department; and the secondary schools, which are administered by the Department of Secondary Education. There are a few special or experimental schools of various types which, as yet, have assumed no great importance in the national programme. In addition, there are the primary schools of the Federal District which are also subject to the Secretariat and are under the control of the Department of Primary and Normal Education of the Federal District.[1]

Federal education has been growing by leaps and bounds in the short period of time that the national programme has been

[1] In addition to the departments indicated, the Secretariat has the Department of Radio Education (and its radio station, XFX); the School Savings Bank; the Office of Publications and Press; the Department of Libraries; the Department of Artistic, Archæological, and Historical Monuments; the Office of Educational Statistics; a Legal Department; the Department of Educational Psychology and Hygiene; the Department of Fine Arts (with its Palace of Fine Arts in Mexico City); and the administrative offices of archives, correspondence, etc.

in operation. By the latter part of 1935 the schools managed by the Rural Department enrolled almost 500,000 children in their day classes and approximately 150,000 adults in night classes. In 1933, immediately prior to the initiation of the Six-Year Plan, there were 7,500 schools of various types. The schools at that time were financed by a budget of 9,500,000 pesos and were directed by 10,300 teachers. By the latter part of 1935 the Rural Department controlled almost 14,000 schools of the various types, employed over 15,000 teachers, and was financed by a budget of more than 14,500,000 pesos. The great majority of the schools are strictly rural and are scattered through every part of the Republic. This makes it necessary that considerable attention be given to the problem of administration and supervision. The following tabulation shows how the personnel of the Department of Rural Education is divided (1935):

| | |
|---|---|
| Technical Board for Rural Education | 5 |
| Department Officials | 27 |
| General Inspectors | 5 |
| State Directors of Education and Administrative Personnel | 189 |
| State Inspectors | 349 |
| Inspector of Indian Boarding Schools | 1 |
| Kindergarten Inspector | 1 |
| Rural Teachers | 12,553 |
| Model and Semi-Urban School Teachers | 1,113 |
| Indian Boarding School Teachers (Approximately) | 120 |
| Teachers in Schools of Article 123 (Schools supported by employers) | 2,447 |
| TOTAL | 16,810 |

Ernest Gruening, in *Mexico and Its Heritage*, says of the total federal appropriation for education in 1927:

But, clearly, an appropriation of some twenty-five million pesos is absurdly inadequate when the job is not merely to sustain an educational plant, but first to create one. As it is, higher education, except for barely maintaining the university and professional schools in the capital, for seven years has been deliberately sacrificed—a decision from which it is difficult to dissent in view of the pressing needs of elementary schooling. Certainly twelve times the present appropriation, which would be approximately the total government revenue, would not constitute an excessive educational outlay for the next generation. Three hundred million pesos would mean a *per capita* expenditure of but twenty pesos—a fair method of estimating, since the task is not merely to educate the children, but the manhood and womanhood of the nation. Obviously, therefore, until economic reconstruction is farther advanced, and Mexico becomes more prosperous, anything beyond a fractional effort is a dream, and a majority of her children will continue as they are today, either without schooling or schooling so slight as to be negligible.

While at present there is less justification for this criticism than there was four years ago, the fact remains that educational opportunity still lags far behind the cultural needs of the nation. Even though the appropriation to the Secretariat of Education exceeded forty-four million pesos in 1935, many times that sum is needed. No matter how sound educational theory may be, the fact remains that a school must have adequate financial support to be wholly successful. It will be many years before Mexico's schools reach the point where the ideals that guide them are no longer seriously impaired by inadequate personnel, insufficient schools, and dearth of materials of instruction.

## Local Initiative

There are dangerous possibilities in the increasing assumption of educational responsibility by the federal government.

Such a policy, if carried to an extreme or if it is put into effect incautiously, may alienate local interest and initiative, thus defeating the very purpose of the schools. The work of the Cultural Missions and other supervisory agencies has done much to develop and keep alive a co-operative attitude among the populace and to relate the school activities to community life. As a matter of fact, financial limitations have made it absolutely necessary that the successful establishment and operation of a school be dependent upon local initiative, support, and co-operation. This healthy outcome of governmental budgetary inadequacy has added tremendously to the local responsibility for schools and has made it possible for them to continue as schools of the people. In addition to this natural development of local initiative, with laudable foresight the Constitution and Laws of the United Mexican States provide specifically for a state of affairs wherein direct responsibility for certain phases of education is placed upon those forces within which the schools are to operate. This is true not only for education but also for other phases of governmental activity.

## Labour Schools of Article 123

Article 123, "The Law of Work" or Labour Article, of the Constitution sets forth the principle that employers are directly responsible for the social and cultural welfare of their employees. In addition to specifications as to hour and wage limits and as to the labour of women and children, this article also provides:

XII. In all agricultural and industrial enterprises, or in any other type of work, the employers are under obligation to make comfortable and hygienic homes available to their workers. . . . They shall also establish schools, infirmaries, and other such services as are necessary to the community. . . .

Laws based on this article, as well as additions to the power of Congress (Article 73) to legislate on the "social welfare," have made it possible for the central government to carry on many of its social reforms by enforcing compliance with the immediate responsibility that employers have towards their workers. Schools which owe their origin to this part of the Constitution are known, both officially and popularly, as "Schools of Article 123."

The educational aspects of Article 123 have resulted in two significant developments. The first is that any employer who, through his industrial or agricultural enterprise, places a group of people under economic dependence on that enterprise is thereby financially responsible for the education of the children of his employees. He must provide a schoolhouse and other necessary material equipment and must pay the salary of one teacher for every fifty (or fraction greater than twenty) children of school age. Oftentimes labour unions supplement the teaching personnel out of their own initiative and funds. Under the provisions of the law, the employer is required to meet the financial responsibilities involved and to turn over the complete control, supervision, and direction of the schools thus established to the federal school system. In other words, his responsibility is social and economic; the administrative and professional responsibility remains with the federal government. A federal law states: "The education that is imparted in such establishments shall be subject to official programmes and to the schools of the federation, and the teachers shall be designated by the federal school authorities. Salaries shall not be less than those assigned to schools of the same level supported by the federal government." Furthermore, it is provided that *patrones* who employ more than four hundred and less than two thousand workers are obligated to establish an advanced fellowship for one of the workers' children so that that student may be able to attend a technical college where training in the industry carried on by that *patrón* is offered. If such an institution is not available in Mexico, the employer is obligated to send the student to some other country for that type of training. The number of such fellowships increases with the increase in employees.

Article 123 sets forth that employers are always in some measure responsible for the welfare of the people who have been made economically dependent upon their business establishments. The responsibility may be expressed through the support of schools, through the founding of infirmaries or recreative establishments, and in other ways. At the same time, elaboration of this article indicates that every large business enterprise has a national responsibility in that the industry is obligated to make trained experts in that type of enterprise available to the Mexican nation. These two responsibilities are over and above the usual civic responsibilities of any individual or organization benefiting by the Mexican society. The political implications of this legislation present interesting possibilities for further discussion and elaboration. Suffice it to say that these laws have contributed greatly to the expansion of the federal system of schools and to the improvement of Mexican education.

The application of Article 123 was left originally to the individual states. Through the efforts of the states, 1,367 Schools of Article 123 were established before January 1934. These schools, as a rule, were an improvement over the state-supported schools. In 1934 the application of the provisions of Article 123 was taken over by the federal government and schools founded under this article were placed under the control of the Secretariat of Education. In 1935 a bureau for these schools was established in the Department of Rural Education and greater efforts were directed towards a better type of school administration and organization. At the present time there are over 2,000 Schools of Article 123. They are managed by 2,500 teachers and the enrolment consists of about 89,000 children and 23,000 adults.

The outstanding examples of this type of school are to be found in connexion with the mining enterprises that are being carried on in various parts of the country. As a general rule the school buildings in these places are superior even to those that are to be found in the large centres of population and compare very favourably with the small-town school buildings in the United States. Construction and equipment are modern and very much in contrast to the inadequate school buildings established by the states and by the federal government. In spite of the many difficulties that are encountered in enforcing the provisions of the law, nearly every large *hacienda*, every textile mill, every mining town, and almost every small community that is economically dependent on some industry boasts of a School of Article 123.

The operation of agrarian reforms and the breaking down of some industries have given rise to considerable opposition to this part of the school programme. It is often puzzling to determine whether or not *campesinos* who have received lands from an *hacienda* are to be regarded as economically dependent on the *hacienda* and whether or not the *hacendado* must not only reduce his enterprise by giving lands but also continue to accept the responsibility of financing a school. This uncertainty has had particularly demoralizing effects in the State of Yucatán, where I have observed schools that were operating on a hand-to-mouth basis, not knowing where to turn for long-overdue teachers' salaries, school-building repairs, assistance in the development of *anexos*, etc. The *hacendado*, already hard pressed by the loss of portions of his best *henequén* fields, feels that his responsibility as an employer has been

lessened by the reduction of his plantation and that it is unjust
to expect him alone to bear a burden that, at least in part,
should now be shifted to his former *peones* or to the people at
large. The government is taking measures to relieve the situation and, with the passage of time, the Schools of Article 123
that find themselves enmeshed in these circumstances will approach the level of efficiency observed for the other schools.
But at present these plantation schools are in a deplorable
state, in direct contrast to schools supported by textile mills,
mines, oil fields, and by other industries not seriously affected
by current socio-economic reforms.

The Schools of Article 123 form an important part of the
national school programme—especially in view of the fact that
they have access to greater financial support than other
federal schools. That is to say, they are where the money is
and they are legally entitled to a share of the wealth produced
by industry from Mexico's resources. As a general rule, these
educational agencies enjoy advantages not found elsewhere and
can carry on their educational and social activities unrestricted
by limited material equipment. They exemplify the principle
that just as the school should fight for social and economic
progress, just so must business enterprises reciprocate by accepting financial responsibility for the welfare of the people,
without whom general economic progress is impossible.

### Wide Scope of the Socialistic Schools

The name "Socialistic Schools" is no longer limited to rural
schools in its application. The secondary schools are socialistic
schools; so are the technical and industrial schools, the rural
normal and agricultural schools, the schools of art and music,
the kindergartens, the city schools—in fact every one of the
many divisions of the Secretariat of Education is consolidated

and integrated with all the others so that the specific functions that any one exercises are related to the functions of the rest to form a programme of action which is the Socialistic School. To such an extent has *La Casa del Pueblo* grown!

The several departments of the Ministry of Education and the educational agencies under their direction are taking steps to spread their influence over the country. The Department of Secondary Education was originally concerned only with secondary schools in the Federal District and in the territories. Within the last three years it has established modern and progressive schools in towns and cities in several parts of the country, particularly in those towns along the border of the United States. Secondary schools at Ciudad Juárez, Nogales, Piedras Negras, and other border towns serve the purpose of competing with the attractions of the American junior and senior high schools across the border, and of giving adolescent boys and girls in these areas the advantages of truly Mexican secondary education. The success which has met the efforts of these border schools has inspired the Department of Secondary Education to establish such schools in other sections of the country.

It is expected that gradually all of Mexican secondary education will be centred in the Secretariat, just as primary or elementary education has practically become a federalized activity managed by the Department of Rural Education. The Mexican *Escuela Secundaria* embraces the grades corresponding to our seventh, eighth, and ninth grades, or to the junior high school. The federal secondary schools seek to co-ordinate academic courses with technical and practical work based on the Mexican economic needs. It is a purpose of these schools to counteract the old type of theoretical, liberal, and verbalist form of instruction imparted by the traditional secondary school. In many respects the *Escuelas Secundarias* are very similar to our American junior high schools, though they are not co-educational and though the Mexican schools have the advantage of being able to encompass within their curricula many phases of social-welfare and community work which are attempted to only a slight extent by American educational institutions.

The federal government, being deeply concerned with the problems of the economic rehabilitation of the middle and lower classes, has sought to make technical training available to young people and has established technical and industrial schools for this purpose. These schools receive boys and girls from either the primary or secondary schools and give them training in fields suitable to their needs and capacities. They offer courses in electricity, various types of shopwork, commerce, domestic science, printing, textile industries, cabinetmaking, and the like. Thousands of boys and girls in the Federal District are taking advantage of the instruction offered by technical and industrial schools that have been in existence there for several years. This type of school is gaining headway in other parts of the country and the number of such schools is growing yearly. Along with these federal technical schools there are those maintained by the states or by municipalities and which prepare boys and girls for useful and remunerative occupations. These trades schools give training in such vocations as tanning, shoemaking and other leather crafts, soapmaking, carpentry and cabinet work, printing, weaving, pottery, and various other small arts and crafts.

The experience of the federal government with the school that was first established under the name of *La Casa del Pueblo* has served it well in setting the pattern for the procedures to be followed in the remainder of the educational ladder and in determining the policy that the government should follow in administering a national system of education. The task of the Socialistic School demonstrates the practicability of co-ordinating the technical function of a school with social action and economic reform. This combination raises the function of the school beyond the mere teaching of subject matter and permits school work to extend into the fields of individual and social hygiene, agricultural and industrial enterprise, home and family life, and all those cultural processes that are related to Mexican life. Questions such as those raised by the prevalence of alcoholism among the *campesinos* and those which are related to the past economic and political exploitation by the Church and other vested interests automatically become provinces for action by the school. In the same manner adult education is as much a responsibility of any of the several types of schools as the instruction of children. The Department of Rural Education specifies that each school must include in its plan of work the following responsibilities in the community:

1. The health of the individual patrons of the school and of the community itself.
2. A thorough understanding of the environment and the way in which that environment may be utilized by the local people.
3. The social and economic phases of home and community life.
4. Popular recreation.

The function of the teachers in the new schools is definitely related to such things as the meetings held by the members of the *ejido,* the activities of workers and labour unions, and the work and processes followed by any and all clubs or groups that have some relation to the welfare of the people. The teachers must make of the school the centre about which revolve all local civic and social enterprises. The schoolhouse then becomes the centre of communal life and the teacher the true leader and guide of communal activities. The teacher's work is divided into three main phases:

1. In the morning he attends to the classroom instruction of children and to the manual activities incident to objective instruction.

2. In the afternoon the teacher guides his pupils in their work in the fields or in those tasks connected with the activities of the *anexos*—the culture of bees, the raising of chickens, the hothouse for fruit trees or for reforestation, and the constructive activities connected with the building of an open-air theatre, toilets, etc. These tasks are concluded with the children's participation in songs, games, and dances. After this period of recreation the children are dismissed as, by this time, the men and women of the village begin to arrive at the school for the adult classes.

3. In the evening this school becomes a place where the adults gather to read the newspapers, to discuss current gossip, and to spend a social hour. At the same time they may also participate in classes in reading, writing, accounting, and elementary agriculture. During his contact with adults the teacher is ever on the lookout for opportunities to inculcate the new socialistic ideas in his patrons and to discuss with them topics of interest that are related to the total national programme.

A former Secretary of Education, Ignacio García Téllez, describes the new schools as follows: "The Socialistic School is: emancipating, unique, obligatory, gratuitous, scientific or rationalistic, technical, of socially useful work, anti-fanatical, and integral." It is possible that the one word in this description that is most vague—integral—is at the same time the one which best interprets the Socialistic School. The new school in Mexico is an integral part of Mexican life and therefore must exhibit those characteristics that are true of life itself. No one word or exposition, however, adequately describes this institution; for, as it operates as a governmental agency in actively participating in and changing the social order, the political and cultural theories on which it is based are all-inclusive. That is to say, the Socialistic School is a school of the environment.

There is no typical Socialistic School, just as there is no standard environment, each community having conditions, needs, attitudes, and social currents peculiar to itself. There is no Socialistic School pattern; only the socialist warp is furnished by the federal government. The source of the woof must be found in each individual situation and the designs and colours must be furnished and worked out by each community. Carrying the analogy still further, the skill and artistic taste exhibited in the weaving process must needs vary in relation to the amount of co-ordination that the individual school is able to achieve between the educative process and community life.

Those of us who are accustomed to schools with more limited responsibilities find it difficult to think of state educational agencies that are actively involved in revolutionary, social, and economic reforms. The people of the United States have never seriously considered the use of their schools as organs for the propagation of "new deal" beliefs, for example, nor as active social forces in contemporary reconstruction. We have zealously protected our schools from the disturbing influences of current problems and have sought to give our children a more or less standardized type of academic education that is carried on in a "purified" school environment, unhampered by the social currents that seethe about them. We jealously guard "states' rights" in education and combat all efforts that smack of federalization of schools. An evaluation of the Socialistic School by Americans must take into consideration, therefore, the existence of vast differences in educational theory between the American and the Mexican schools in these fundamental aspects.

It is fairly easy to compare Mexican and American schools in terms of their material aspects. Yet, in any objective comparison it would be impossible and unjust to leave out the subjective elements which are the directing force. For example, American school buildings in general are far superior to the makeshift plants commonly found in Mexico. However, the adobes and timbers used in the construction of the Mexican classroom have been donated by an impoverished people, and the labour that has gone into the construction represents a personal contribution of the members of the community rather than a service that has been bought and paid for. In Mexico the methods of instruction and the educative activities of the school are not carried on in a purified environment but form a part of the natural and real-life processes within the life of a community. It is preferable, then, to think of the new schools in old Mexico in relation to the total life of Mexico, past and present, rather than in relation to the school as an isolated institution. To appreciate the Socialistic School it is necessary that one first know and understand Mexican historical development, the geographic setting, the social and economic problems of Mexico, and the hopes and aspirations that four hundred years of strife have instilled in the Mexican. The Socialistic School is "integral" and represents a socio-economic process more than an educational process, as we commonly understand the phrase in the United States.

The Socialistic School is rational; yet it owes its existence to a spiritual and emotional demand. It is revolutionary, symbolizing a general dissatisfaction with what has existed and reflecting an intolerance of the conditions forced upon the people by centuries of social and economic maladjustment. With due allowances for the administrative and political deficiencies which may be observed in the Socialistic School, this is the agency that best represents the present Mexican ideal.

# CHAPTER VII

# TEACHER-TRAINING AND INDIAN SCHOOLS

T HE preparation of teachers is one of the vital factors in any educational system. This has always been recognized in Mexico. From the time when Fray Pedro de Gante trained assistants to aid him in his teaching duties up until the present, teacher-training institutions have carried on educational activities second in importance only to those of the primary schools. I believe that it can be safely said that these normal schools have contributed more to the cultural advancement of Mexico than any other single educational institution of secondary or higher grade. As early as the middle of the nineteenth century, practically every capital city and large centre of population boasted a primary normal school. These schools were accessible to a large portion of the population and, as more advanced schools were not readily available,[1] the normal schools became not only institutions for the training of teachers but centres of advanced secondary education for the population in general.

The normal schools served as centres for the advanced training of many Mexicans who were to become leaders in the political affairs of the nation and in other fields of Mexican

---

[1] It should not be ignored that Mexico has had universities and technical, professional, and liberal colleges for many years. These, together with the military colleges, still form the upper rung of the educational ladder. They are not specifically treated in this report because they, and their respective preparatory schools, are not directly involved in the new educational movement and as yet form no part of the programme of the Secretariat of Education. The national colleges, with the exception of the autonomous National University of Mexico, are administered by other Secretariats.

life. These schools were, in effect, general colleges rather than specialized professional schools. However, the fact that those who attended these institutions for general college purposes were at the same time exposed to the professional educational courses has had very beneficial results in the attitude taken by political leaders towards the educational growth of the Republic. It has been characteristic of Mexican politics that schools have always received consideration when political reforms and the cultural emancipation of the masses have been proposed. All reform movements, from the time of Independence to date, have been deeply tinged with recognition of the important part that schools should play in national affairs. Even today, when it might be expected that the career of the educator would be clearly differentiated and his activities fairly well delimited, it is surprising to note the ease with which both schoolmen and statesmen carry on either political or educational activities with equal insight and efficiency. It could well be said that, generally speaking, the educated Mexican statesman is also an educator and that, conversely, the educator is so directly concerned with and informed on political affairs that he can, and often does, become the statesman. The normal school in Mexico, with all its deficiencies as a professional or even as an academic institution, has served Mexico well in correlating civic thought with educational development.

The normal schools before 1880 reflected the formalism and artificiality of education in general for that period. They were purely academic institutions wherein students acquired "book learning" through courses that had very little relation to the real problems in Mexican life. With a few exceptions, this condition continued up until the time when the new federal normal schools were created. Nevertheless, as early as the middle of the nineteenth century there was evidence of dissatisfaction with the programme of the teacher-training centres. During the reform movement of 1857–1872, the victory of the liberal forces led by Benito Juárez was reflected in attempts by statesmen and educators to relate the work of the normal schools to the problems of the people. Because there was only a handful of rural schools in existence and as the normal schools were situated in the centres of population, the teacher-training agencies were concerned chiefly with the preparation of teachers for urban schools. Nevertheless, in spite of the cultural limitations of their situation, some of their activities at that time showed a tendency to turn away from the stilted education of the past and towards greater appreciation of the kind of school programme that was suited to local needs.

The brilliant efforts of the Swiss educator, Rébsamen, mark the beginnings of a new period in teacher-training—a period that may be designated as "modern" in that the procedures and methods which he advocated compare favourably with those in common use today in Mexico and elsewhere. The experimental schools which he established, the practice and demonstration primary schools which he created in connexion with his normal schools, and the revisions which he introduced into the normal-school curriculum sought to vitalize teacher-training. The part that Rébsamen played in national councils guided educational thought in Mexico into a new period of reform. The liberal movement in education which he presented, together with Justo Sierra and others, combined with the liberal political attitude of such leaders as Juárez and his followers, laid the groundwork for the reaction which has contributed so much to the departure in education which we witness today.

It was inevitable that, although some of the normal schools reflected an advance over the educational thought of the past, they were sorely limited by the conditions under which they worked. Rural education, as such, did not exist in Mexico before 1920. Urban culture was not Mexican culture but represented a poor imitation of mannerisms and ideas that had been borrowed from foreign nations. In the midst of these conditions, even the better normal schools were unable to prepare teachers to meet the needs of the masses of the Mexican people. The valiant efforts of the national normal schools in the Federal District and those of the normal schools founded by Rébsamen in the States of Veracruz, Oaxaca, Guanajuato, and elsewhere were not sufficient to break down the barriers raised by a prevailing culture that did not reflect the hopes and needs of the peoples of Mexico. The National Teachers' College,[2] which arose from the early normal schools in the Federal District, today vouches for the advance that some normal schools had made in seeking to direct Mexico towards the new movement in education. Leading educators from the world over have visited this institution and have marvelled at the progressive educational thought and practice that is to be found there—this in spite of the well-known curtailment that has taken place in the activities in this institution within recent years.

Admitting that certain of the normal schools, especially the National Teachers' College, had made contributions to progressive thought, the fact remains that true Mexican education had been almost completely neglected by the normal schools up to the time of the rise of the new schools in 1921. In those rare instances where normal schools did prepare teachers adequately, the immensity of the problem nullified

---

[2] This college and the primary schools of the Federal District are administered by the Secretariat of Education through its Department of Primary and Normal Education of the Federal District.

their efforts. A nation-wide system of teacher-training, suited to the type of education the Mexican people needed, did not exist. Normal schools were concerned chiefly with preparing individuals to enter the verbalist classrooms of city schools. Their graduates were devoted to book knowledge and artificial culture and had little concept of the real task that confronted the Mexican teacher.

Under these conditions it is not surprising that, when the Secretariat of Education undertook the task of founding rural schools in 1921, suitably trained teachers were not available. Not only was there an insufficient number of normal-school graduates who might have been drafted into the service but these *normalistas* were as incapable of coping with the rural problem as the most untrained laymen. The newly created Secretariat had the insight and the courage to discard this source of teachers and to venture into the undertaking with raw material that at least had the advantage of susceptibility to the influence of the revolutionary spirit that guided the creation of new schools. The Federal Office of Education was forced by circumstances to accept as teachers for the new schools persons whose only qualification lay in that they showed some inclination to enter into the new venture and that they needed a job. Many of the first teachers were *normalistas* but the great majority had been picked up more or less indiscriminately. This is true also of the early *misioneros* although these, in addition to meeting some professional prerequisites, had been selected for personal qualities that were evidence of a peculiar capacity for their missionary duties. This personnel deficiency could not be permitted to impede the march that the Secretariat had started towards a cultural revolution. At the same time, a recognition of this deficiency made it necessary that the federal government assume the responsibility for developing a new source of teachers.

## Rural Normal Schools

At the outset the Secretariat sought to make use of a type of normal school which, unfortunately, took the institutions of the time as a pattern and which was not well suited to the rural field. Since all normal-school training up to that time had in mind only the preparation of teachers for city schools, it soon became apparent that a new type of normal school had to be created. The new kind of training school needed a rural setting—an environment that was similar to what rural teachers would encounter in the field. Fresh types of educational courses also had to be offered by these normal schools—courses that would have rural life as their base. With this in view, the present method of procedure was decided upon and in 1926 several Rural Normal Schools were established. These schools dedicated themselves to the task of preparing the children of peasants for teaching positions among peasants. They made themselves into a rural community, with agricultural grounds and conditions similar to those of the neighbouring villages. They accepted students who had either an "elementary-primary" (4th grade) or a "superior-primary" (6th grade) education. In spite of the prejudice that existed in the cities against co-education, the normal schools recognized that men and women teachers were going to teach side by side when they went into the villages and that, therefore, the normal schools should be co-educational.

The Mexican Rural Normal School today can be considered an older brother of the rural primary school. Normal-school students are placed in situations very similar to those in which they will place their children in village primary schools. The management of the institution is in the hands of the students. The student body divides itself into commissions for tasks ranging from the preparation of meals to the administration of co-operative marketing organizations and school government. As the school is situated away from the centres of population, it has of necessity become a boarding school in which teachers and pupils live as one great rural family. There is always a primary school in connexion with each normal school. This *primaria* forms an *anexo* to the normal school and serves as the observation and practice school for the future teachers. The building in which the normal school is housed may be an abandoned church or convent or some ruined *hacienda* that has been restored by the pupils themselves. The activities of the normal school, both academic and manual, are carried on in a spirit of co-operation and in such a natural way that the professional preparation which results is in no way hindered by that formality and artificiality which is too often characteristic of teacher-training institutions elsewhere. The faculty of a Rural Normal School is made up of:

A Director, who is also in charge of some professional courses
A woman in charge of domestic economy of the boarding school
A physician
An agriculture teacher
A teacher of education courses
Three instructors of general subjects
Three shop teachers
A physical-education director
Various clerical assistants

The teacher-training course was limited originally to one year as, more often than not, the first year of the two years of preparation had to be devoted to completing the students' elementary education. Gradually the length of professional courses has been extended, first to two years and in some institutions to three. It has been accepted that the preparation of teachers involves not only instruction in professional courses

but also both general and specific education that is directed
at the problems of rural Mexico. The curriculum of the Rural
Normal Schools includes:

> Agricultural Practices
> Arithmetic and Geometry
> Art
> Domestic Science
> Educational Psychology
> Literature
> Music
> National Language (Spanish)
> Natural Science
> Observation and Practice Teaching
> Physical Education
> Physics and Chemistry
> Physiology and Hygiene
> Principles of Education
> Regional Indian Language
> Rural School Administration
> Rural Social Organization
> Social Sciences
> Techniques of Teaching
> Trades and Industries

It might be said that the fundamental aim of rural normal
schools in Mexico is that of grounding prospective teachers in
the social and economic problems of rural Mexico in terms of
the part that the village schools are to play in solving these
problems. The necessity for training teachers in the type of
economic activities in which the peasants engage, chiefly agriculture and the small industries related to farming, is apparent. The teacher must know how to use a forge just as well as
he can use a blackboard. While it is necessary that he become
proficient in the academic fields, it is of still greater impor-

tance that he be prepared to become a leader in the social and economic practice of the village in which he is to work. He must be capable of utilizing the rural environment for cultural purposes and of relating his formal school programme to the daily habits and labours of the people. He must know the aims and purposes of the federal government and must be ready to interpret current social and economic reconstruction to the patrons of his school. The Rural Normal School is placed in a rural setting, it has the children of peasants for students, its practices are not unlike those to be found in the *rancherías, haciendas,* and *ejidos*—in effect, the Rural Normal School is a part of what heretofore had been "Forgotten Mexico." Its task is that of bringing to "barbarous" Mexico a cultural institution that is peculiarly suited to fit the *indio* and *campesino* to fight for their own redemption.

In 1932 there were 17 Rural Normal Schools, located in as many states. Since that time some of these have been converted into "Regional Rural Schools," which will be discussed shortly. In 1935 only 11 Rural Normal Schools existed under that name. These enrolled 1,193 students, of whom 819 were boys and 374 were girls. Every effort has been made to place these teacher-training institutions in agricultural areas that are typical of the region, so that the agricultural practices and the general environment of the school may fit into the total picture and so that the students may be able to carry on practices that are not foreign to the communities among which they are to teach. Living conditions in the normal schools echo the standard of living of the region and are not far removed, if at all, from the primitive culture of the peasants of that section of the country. The Rural Normal Schools of Mexico serve their functions as teacher-training institutions and cultural missions by adapting themselves to the conditions and needs of those whom they are to enlighten.

### Agricultural Schools

One of the first attempts of the revolutionary government to improve farming in the country was through the establishment of agricultural schools. Several of these were opened between 1925 and 1932 in various sections of the country under the Federal Secretariat of Agriculture. As there was no satisfactory precedent for this type of school in Mexico, the newly created schools turned to the agricultural and technical colleges of the United States and other nations for their pattern. They were fortunate in having adequate funds at their disposal and they began their work by introducing modern methods of agriculture into Mexico. They copied the method of procedure of the American schools. They introduced pure-bred animals and complicated farm machinery. At one stroke they sought to raise Mexican agriculture from a medieval stage to the level of the twentieth century. These schools failed and failed miserably. Their methods and their materials were in no way suited to the needs of Mexican agriculture. They were as foreign to real life in Mexico as the academic instruction of the old normal schools had been in the teacher-training field. They sought to standardize Mexican agriculture by means of modern innovations for which Mexico was not ready and which, in many cases, were of no practical advantage to Mexican agriculture. Little differentiation was made between the agricultural instruction required by a student from the high barren wastes of northern Mexico and that required by a student who was going to farm in the tropical swamps of the south-east.

I have visited agricultural schools where the tractors and gang ploughs that were to replace the oxen and the Egyptian plough now lie abandoned in rust and neglect. I have heard how the pure-bred chickens, pigs, horses, and cows which were

imported from foreign countries have fallen victims to the
rigours of climate and to the inroads of local insects and dis-
eases. The failure of these transplanted agricultural colleges
demonstrated conclusively that Mexico's salvation must be
accomplished by an application of Mexican means and methods. The ideal value of the innovations introduced by the
*"Centrales Agrícolas,"* as the agricultural schools were known,
is fully appreciated, but it has been concluded that these advantages can be utilized only when proper recognition is made
of the peculiar situation that rural Mexico and the *campesino*
occupy in the scheme of Mexican life. This experience again
demonstrated that economic progress must go hand in hand
with cultural enlightenment and that the two must be built on
indigenous conditions.

In 1932 the agricultural schools were turned over by the
Secretariat of Agriculture to the Secretariat of Education. By
that time the enrolment had decreased to about 50 per cent
of capacity. The Federal Office of Education immediately began an intensive campaign to utilize these new agencies in its
established educational programme. The faculty of the schools
was reorganized and their courses changed to meet general
educational needs in agriculture rather than specialized technical instruction. The schools were placed under the direction
of the Department of Rural Normal Schools and Cultural
Missions. This action in itself indicated the trend which the
office of education sought to follow in incorporating the agricultural schools into the federal educational system. At that
time there were seven *Centrales Agrícolas,* situated in the agricultural regions of several parts of the country. Two more
were added shortly afterwards. By changing the system of internal organization, by modifying the entrance requirements,
by introducing educational ideas that had already been tested
in rural normal schools, and by giving these new additions to

the federal system a more socializing tendency, it was believed
that they would be able to serve rural Mexico. As early as
1932 the Department of Rural Normal and Agricultural
Schools of the Secretariat had in mind that the agricultural
schools should play an important part not only in preparing
practical farmers among the peasants but also in assisting in
the task of training rural teachers. These new agencies were
admirably equipped as boarding schools, having innumerable
conveniences which were not and still are not available to the
regular rural normal schools. The chief aim in the reorgani-
zation of agricultural schools was to adapt them to practical
rural life and to make them a part of the rural school revolution.

### Growth of Regional Training Schools

The success obtained by the rural normal schools has already been noted. However, federal officials were well aware
that these schools were serving merely as agencies which in
a very elementary manner introduced unprepared primary-
school graduates into both the teaching and agricultural fields.
It might be said that the rural normal schools represented the
first grade in teacher-training and in agricultural instruction.
With the acquisition of the agricultural schools by the Secretariat, the Directors of Rural Normal Schools, the Directors of
Federal Education, and the heads of the *Centrales Agrícolas*
saw the opportunities opened by the new additions. A confer-
ence of these officials, during the latter part of 1932, recom-
mended that the programmes of rural normal schools and of
agricultural schools be combined and that existing agricultural
and normal schools be designated as "Regional Rural Schools"
which would perform both agricultural and teacher-training
functions. Since that time six of the nine agricultural schools
and three rural normal schools have become Regional Rural

Schools. Today there are only three *Centrales Agrícolas* and eleven Rural Normal Schools. By the end of 1936 all of these will be converted into Regional Rural Schools and, with the addition of five regional schools that are already partly under way, there will be twenty-eight such schools in the nation before the end of 1936.

The regional schools are destined to become the general colleges of rural education. Their programme extends over a three-year period. The first two years are devoted to basic elementary courses in the fields of social science, agriculture, education, national and Indian languages, farm practices, small industries, and the like. Those who are to follow either farming or teaching careers participate in the courses of the first two years indiscriminately. The third year is devoted to greater specialization in teacher-training and in agriculture. Those who are preparing themselves as teachers take more advanced courses in teaching methods and principles of educational organization while those who seek specialization in agriculture receive more advanced training in courses suited to that division. It is intended that the enrolment be limited to boys and girls who have completed the sixth grade of elementary education, but provisions are made so that those with only the elementary-primary training (fourth grade) are also received.

The activities of the rural regional schools are modelled much after the procedures followed in rural normal schools. There are co-operative societies and commissions for every phase of school life. The students take an active part in the management of the institution and carry on all of the agricultural enterprises of the school, much as if they were all members of a communal enterprise—which is essentially the situation. The school is organized into a Cultural Mission and the social action of the school is a major phase of the school life.

Various commissions and expeditions keep in contact with the villages in the region surrounding the school, instituting reforms and improvements much as the Cultural Missions do. Definite responsibility is placed upon the student body for the improvement of rural conditions in the vicinity. Students have many opportunities to display qualities of leadership in real-life situations and they are guided into attacking local problems in a natural way and as members of the social group. These activities are of great interest to the students and become a very effective part of their training. From the observation of different groups, who were engaged in such diverse tasks as sweeping the streets of a neighbouring village and presenting a musical festival to the *campesinos*, I am convinced that this phase of their training is the one of greatest value to them as citizens and as teachers or farmers. The happy combination of agricultural training and teacher-preparation and the possibilities presented by social action in real-life situations lay the groundwork for skill and enthusiasm on the part of the students in reaching into the very heart of those conditions which must be overcome in reforming rural Mexico.

It was originally intended that the regional schools should have a fourfold function:

1. Normal (teacher-training) Instruction
2. Agricultural-Industrial Education
3. Social and Economic Investigation and Research
4. Social Action through a Cultural Mission

The last two of these phases have not been added owing to financial limitations, although the third phase is being carried on by supervisors who serve regions where new regional schools are to be established. In a sense, however, all four phases are in operation for, though the last two have not been formally organized, the studies and investigations of student groups and the socializing activities which they undertake in the neighbourhood fill the gaps that would otherwise be evident in the educational programme of the institution.

Only the best students are permitted to remain for the third or final year of the regional-school course, whether it be in-education or agriculture. Children of *ejidatarios* and children who come from small farms are given preference in enrolment. The federal government pays for all the necessary school costs of the pupils—clothing, food, shelter, medical attention, etc. It also provides inducements for those who remain for the final year of instruction. If a student has majored in agriculture, upon graduation he is rewarded by a *"dotación"*— agricultural lands and the minimum essentials in material equipment. If he is graduated in education, he is assured of a teaching position in one of the federal schools. All students are sons or daughters of *campesinos*. The agricultural practices that are carried on in the school and the small industries in which the students engage serve in part to pay the expenses of operation and to create funds which are placed to the credit of the students. These funds are distributed to the students upon graduation and constitute a financial resource which is to aid them in their future work as teachers or farmers.

The number of teacher-training centres is far from adequate for a federal school programme that is making so phenomenal a growth. There is little likelihood that a balance will be established between teacher supply and demand for many years to come. Many more regional rural schools are contemplated at present, but even if the existing number were doubled within the next two or three years, they could not possibly meet the growing need for trained rural teachers. This means that the federal school programme is going to have to depend to a great extent upon the teachers who are selected from the ranks of the general population. This also means that the task of in-service training of teachers will continue to be of great importance. The rural school teacher himself assumes greater importance in the scheme of education in view of the fact that the graduates of primary schools will continue to step into teaching positions without further preparation.

## Indian Education

One of the greatest accomplishments of the Revolution is observed in the attention that has been directed towards the problems of the Indian population. Before 1910 little was heard of that vast group of Mexicans that still constitutes more than one-fourth of the total population and that has been in a state of complete neglect for more than four hundred years. Not only were they isolated by the clash of cultures but, in self-defence, the Mexican Indian retreated into inaccessible regions and avoided the social and economic changes that were taking place in other parts of Mexico. The Revolution of 1910 gave the oppressed *indio* an opportunity to give vent to the hatred which centuries of injustice had developed within him. The part he played in the Revolution demonstrated to the country as a whole that the Indian demanded national recognition and that his problems were an important part of life in Mexico.

While the Revolution of 1910 was a *mestizo* movement, it was essentially a movement by the underprivileged classes in which were included the Indian masses. In a very real sense the Indian made victory possible and it was fitting that the "men of the Revolution" should seek to reward his efforts and to extol the contributions that he had made and could continue to make in Mexico's growth. Whereas, in the past, the *indio* had been despised and ostracized, the Revolution gave rise to a feeling which glorified and exalted everything that was Indian. Many *mestizo* revolutionaries proudly boast, "I am Indian." Rather than being a disgrace, today it is a privilege to be an Indian or, if this is not possible, to attach oneself to the cause of the Mexican Indian. After four centuries of slavery the *indio* is coming into his own. While the material handicaps to his economic and cultural redemption are many, the fundamental basis on which such a redemption may be achieved has been established through the acceptance of the equality, and possibly the superiority, of the Indian as a member of the Mexican nation. Because he was despoiled, exploited, and stupefied in the past, it devolves upon the Revolution to make restitution to the *indio* and to campaign for his redemption.

Even as late as 1925 a great many people in Mexico doubted the capacity of the Indian to become a valuable member of the Mexican society. Many people believed that the despised *indio* was not worthy of consideration as an equal and certainly could not profit by a cultural programme. To satisfy this doubt, ridiculous as it was, more evidence was needed to disprove the fallacy that had been bred by several hundred years of indifference to this lowest caste of Mexican society. It was difficult for the Mexican people to believe that these human beasts of burden, these "stupid" human cattle, these traditional slaves, deserved the attention of the cultural revolution that was under way. It was necessary that an experiment be set up to demonstrate to an incredulous populace that the Mexican Indian was capable of receiving and utilizing the benefits of an education.

In 1925 the Secretariat of Education established the now famous *"Casa del Estudiante Indígena"* ("House of the Indigenous Student") in Mexico City. Pure-blood Indian boys, from the different tribes in various parts of the Republic, were brought to this school and given both a general and a vocational education. They came from isolated Indian villages, knowing almost nothing of Western culture, speaking native dialects, and personifying the primitive stage of their respective communities. Tarahumaras from the barren wastes of Chihuahua, Mayas from the limestone plains of Yucatán, Totonacas from the mountain heights of the Sierra Madre Oriental, Huicholes, Yaquis, Otomíes, Mixtecas—representatives of nearly all groups were selected by the school officials and by the local chiefs and sent in their distinctive and picturesque garb to cosmopolitan Mexico City. The boys were taken in hand by the teachers of the school and given a fundamental education. Through various types of shopwork the Indian boys were taught trades and industries which would make them capable of earning a living in their villages or elsewhere. They held athletic contests; they presented festivals where Indian culture was illustrated and glorified; they were placed in contact with all the cultural influences that abound in the capital of the country and, in effect, they were given the best that the Mexican cultural institutions of the present could offer any young man of that educational level.

The boys took advantage of their opportunities and were soon able to demonstrate that they were fully capable of competing with other students in other schools in any of the activities of current education. If one criticism can be made of the House of the Indigenous Student, it is that this school did its work too well. Graduates of the school had been prepared to fit into Mexican society, but they had been educated out of their traditional environment and were made foreigners to their own people. It could not be hoped that young men with the training and vocational preparation that these young men had obtained would be willing to return to the primitive conditions from which they came or, if they did return, that they would remain in their native homes. A primitive village in the parched mountains of northern Chihuahua presented no attraction to a well-educated young Tarahumara who had, by the grace of the Indian School, become an expert auto-mechanic or who was proficient in the use of complicated tanning machinery. Even if the vocation which he had learned could have been carried on with profit in his native home, greater horizons had been opened to him by his education and he had no incentive to sacrifice himself on the frontiers of culture. The rehabilitation of individuals could have little effect on the miserable status of more than four million of their brethren. Nevertheless, the school had proved its point—the Mexican Indian could and did profit by modern education.

Paradoxically, in so far as the cultural revolution was concerned, in spite of its success as an educational centre the House had served a purpose counter to the end in view. As an educational agency it served as a centre of disintegration in that it disconnected the Indian leaders whom it trained from the problems of their people. To correct this, the school was given a teacher-training function in 1928. From that time until its close in 1932 the school served as an agency which prepared young men for teaching positions in Indian villages. In this way the students were given an incentive to return to their homes. Through this change the work of the institution was more closely related to the needs of backward Indian peoples scattered over the country. Even so, it became clear that the purposes which the House had in view could be carried on much better if its functions were assigned to agencies that were in closer contact with the homes of the various peoples whom schools of this nature were to serve. Professor Rafael Ramírez has said: "So we set about looking for more satisfactory methods that would integrate the Indians by groups and masses and not by individuals and, above all, that when they became integrated with civilized groups they should not become alienated from their intrinsic ideals and worthy types of life. . . . The educational experiment brought about through the House of the Indigenous Student was not a failure. Everybody in

Mexico is now convinced that it is possible to educate the Indian because it is recognized that he has great capacity, and not only are we convinced of this truth but also of the urgent necessity to do so."

With the budget that had heretofore been assigned to the House of the Indigenous Student, the Secretariat of Education in 1933 created ten *"Centros de Educación Indígena"*—"Centres of Indigenous Education." Each one of these centres was situated in the very heart of the Indian area where each was to serve and every centre was made to reflect, in so far as possible, the culture of the peoples in that area. They were designated as "centres" rather than "schools" because it was intended that education should come through a natural participation in those social and economic activities which were suited to the people and the region rather than through formal or academic instruction. Instead of being simply Indian boarding schools (for pure-blood boys and girls of ages fourteen to twenty and twelve to twenty, respectively) these centres were also to become the focus for the cultural incorporation of the Indian communities of the area. The material equipment of an *internado indígena*, or Indian boarding school, is rustic and represents a level only slightly in advance of that of the local communities. Every effort is put forth to make the transition from primitive culture to the school environment as gradual and flexible as possible. Each boarding school has extensive agricultural grounds. Small shops and industries, related to an agricultural life, form a medium through which the educational influences of the school are imparted. The school's activities are very similar to those in which the child would normally engage, though they are purposefully guided in such manner that the student is led along by almost imperceptible stages. By the end of 1934 the following new Indian schools had been established:

Three in the Tarahumara region of Chihuahua
Two in the Indian region of Guerrero
One in the Mixteca region of Oaxaca
One among the Otomíes of Querétaro
One for the Totonacas of Puebla
One among the Chamulas of Chiapas
One among the Mazaguas of México
One in the Huasteca area of San Luis Potosí
One among the Mayas of Yucatán

During 1935 ten more centres were put into operation in nine different states and the groundwork laid for five more. Each one of the centres enrols about fifty boys and girls and is in the charge of a faculty composed of a director of the school, an elementary teacher, six vocational teachers, and a nurse. The centre functions as a large family, the only formality observed being that of instruction of the students in school work ranging from the first through the fourth grade. Though the class work is definitely provided for and scheduled, it is so arranged that it is not permitted to interfere with the important social and vocational functions of the institution. Student government plays an important part and all activities are carried on by co-operative commissions so that every individual is definitely related to every phase of school life— whether it be in tilling the fields, in preparing and serving meals, in constructing buildings and annexes, or in social-welfare work in the villages.

It is not intended that the Indian boarding schools should take the place of the regular rural schools but, instead, they are to supplement the work of these and reach more intimately into the life of the Indian population. Because of their strategic location, they are able to impart education in the indigenous environment itself and are able to take advantage of the educational influences that radiate from Indian society. Since they are co-educational and since the students are received by the school long before they reach maturity and are kept there over a period of several years, the *internados* are able to exercise a strong guiding influence over the future lives of the pupils. Whereas the regular rural school is constantly confronted with the restricting influence of the home environment, the *internados* are admirably situated to guide their students gradually away from a low standard of living and an inferior cultural life to higher planes without great shock and without alienating the Indian boys and girls from their people. As a general rule, each centre has a primary rural school in conjunction and the operation of this school is associated closely with the activities of the centre. The fundamental purposes for which these Indian schools have been established may be stated as follows: (1) to rehabilitate Indian groups socially and economically; (2) to promote, stimulate, and direct their progress and to integrate them spiritually into the level of culture in which the inhabitants of the rest of the country are found in order that Mexico may be a socially unified nation; (3) to make them Hispanic in language and, thereby, help to give Mexico a single language.

Every phase of the work of the Indian boarding schools has some social significance and the performance of every task is dignified with cultural values in some aspect of rural life. From the very moment that the school is opened for the first time, its entire programme rests upon the combined efforts of teachers and pupils. The building is constructed by them; they plough and plant the fields; they make their own beds and clothes; and, with the exception of teachers' salaries and the few centavos the federal government pays for each student *per diem*, the plant is operated entirely through the work of the faculty and the students.

At the *Internado Indígena Totonaca* at Zongozotla in the

State of Puebla, the boys and girls explained to me how they exchanged services adapted to their respective interests. For example, two boys would construct the wooden bed for a girl student while she in turn made the clothing for the boys. Whereas, before coming to school, the students were accustomed to sleeping on the bare ground in most unhygienic conditions, at the school they learn the advantages and comforts of beds constructed by themselves and of clothing better adapted to the climate and to their labours. An old graveyard has been levelled off and made into a fine basketball court. The abandoned stable of the church has been converted into a shop where musical instruments are manufactured. The school proper is housed in an old village-government house. The girls prepare savoury and well-balanced meals from the products of the farm while the boys engage in the heavier tasks of the school-community. As the girls will return to villages where they are expected by tradition to participate in farm tasks, little distinction is made between the agricultural practices of boys and girls. Villagers find the *internado* a place of great interest and one where attention will be given to whatever problems confront them. The little *fiestas* at the school are a source of great delight to every one. Music, dances, recitations, orations, and harmless merry-making of all sorts add a breath of joy and happiness to an existence that would otherwise be drab and miserable.

During my visit at this school a threatened *Cristero* raid had a surprising effect upon the Indians of the surrounding villages. The school was armed and the villagers constituted themselves into vigilance groups to be ready at the first call to defend their *internado* with their lives. The threats of bloody attacks by the rebels did not demoralize the school nor affect its daily routine. Naturally, all were on the *qué vive* and firearms were much in evidence day and night. Yet the school had demonstrated its value so well to the Indians that, had the threatened raid materialized, I believe that victory would have gone to the supporters of the school even though the *Cristeros* were reputed to number more than seventy-five.

At Comaltepec, in the same state, I witnessed the early steps in the establishment of a boarding school for Aztecs. Both teachers and pupils were sleeping on the ground under make-shift shelters or in the abandoned rooms of the adjoining church. Pupils and teachers were working on plans for the shops, for additional buildings, etc. The chiefs of near-by villages visited the school constantly to confer about prospective students, to get advice on farming, health, and other local problems. The director of the school was taking steps to make medical attention available to the people in view of the prevalence of goitre which temporarily had been diagnosed as resulting from a deficiency in the local water supply. The Indians of this region, as well as those near Zongozotla, while normally difficult to meet and loath to talk to strangers, showed great delight in discussing their rural schools and their beloved *internados*.

The Otomí students at the Indian boarding school, "Cuauhtémoc," at Quitiyé in the State of Querétaro, are illustrations of the effectiveness of this school programme. In contrast to their relatives in the surrounding villages, who appear dull and stupid and who avoid contacts with Western culture, the young men and women at Quitiyé exhibit remarkable qualities of co-operation and a burning desire to learn. Even though they had but recently been introduced to the Spanish language, they showed a keen interest also in learning a few English words and in hearing about far places. They had renovated and reconstructed an abandoned *hacienda* which is an architectural beauty, among the best that I have seen in the Republic. Painstakingly they have rebuilt walls, turrets, guard .

houses, flower gardens, and sun porches, and have adapted the plan of the old mansion admirably to the purposes of a school-community. In spite of the many things accomplished in resurrecting the beauties of the *hacienda* and in agricultural pursuits in the fields, the most striking note of the *internado* is to be found in the alertness of the children and the devotion of the teachers. The students take advantage of every opportunity to extend the influence of the school into the neighbouring communities and, though they regret the thought of leaving the happy home which the school has become, they turn eager eyes to the day when they may offer the force of their faith and devotion and their newly acquired talents to the solution of the problems of their people.

Most of the students of the *internados* return to their home villages after leaving school and almost automatically become "wise men" among their people. They become the source from which emanates the culture which has been so carefully nurtured at the school. They establish themselves in the community and, not being content with a primitive standard of home life, they introduce practical innovations which set the example for their neighbours. The abler students, as a rule, go to a near-by rural normal school to prepare for the teaching profession. Today many of the rural teachers are of pure Indian blood. It is the hope of the Secretariat of Education that many more Indians will go into the teaching profession so that they can be the medium through which the cultural revolution will be carried on among the Indian peoples. It should not be understood, however, that the Secretariat is depending entirely upon Indians for rural education among Indians. Students at rural normal schools are studying local Indian languages so that they may be better able to reach the centre of community life when they assume charge of a rural school in an Indian region. It should be repeated that rural schools are established with preference in Indian regions and that the *internados* are intended as supplementary institutions and do not displace the regular rural school.

In the education of Indians as well as in the total school programme, the new federal movement in education has been able to achieve surprising results. Even so, it must be said that it is yet too early to judge the efficacy of the new schools. There are still many regions to which the new movement has not penetrated and there are large groups of Indians and *mestizos* who have yet to taste the fruits which the cultural revolution is seeking to place within their reach. The accomplishments of a scant fifteen years have gone a long way towards bringing all of Mexico into the educational fold, but much is yet to be done. Many more schools are needed if every region is to be served. While it is true that great masses of children are now enjoying the privileges of the primary school, there are still large numbers who have not been introduced to the cultural advantages to which they are entitled by virtue of the victory by revolution. From practically every point of view, the new movement in Mexican education must be considered, for the time being, as an experimental one. What has been accomplished up until the present should be viewed in the light of results from a pioneering venture. While this venture has already presented much evidence of promise and while there can be no doubt that the masses of the people have profited greatly as a result of what has already been accomplished in education, the real test of the school programme still lies in the future.

### Promising Features of Teacher-Training

Devotion and inspiration on the part of her teachers have served Mexico well so far, but the permanent success of a federal system of education will make further demands of those who are to conduct the activities of the classroom. The interest which the government is showing in the establishment of teacher-training institutions is evidence of its understanding that future work must be grounded on a sound professional base. It will be some time before these efforts result in a balance between supply and demand in trained teaching personnel. To the extent that such a balance is achieved, to that extent will Mexico free herself from complete dependence upon faith and devotion which, taken alone, offer doubtful permanence to the cultural revolution.

The new teacher-training programme presents several phases that are worthy of special emphasis. In the first place, Mexico has sought to use the evangelical spirit found among the masses of the people. The sons and daughters of *campesinos* are the ones who are being selected as the future teachers of their people. They, more than any one else, are in tune with the rhythm that is Mexico and they are best qualified to sympathize with the hopes and the needs of the masses whom the federal government is pledged to serve. In the second place, the teacher-training institutions themselves have been bound closely to Mexican soil and have been directly related, socially and economically, to the regions and the peoples to be affected by their graduates. Not only do they seek to meet their teacher-training responsibilities but they also seek to prepare their students in those activities and points of view which will make it possible for them to participate actively in the cultural enlightenment of the *campesino* and in his social and economic rehabilitation. The normal schools, through their very organization and location, insinuate themselves into the environment of rural Mexico, becoming a part of that environment. In no sense are they alien institutions but their every effort is to bring about change and growth in a natural manner. In the third place, Mexico's normal schools are cultural missions as well. They are active agents striving for the social and economic welfare of the peoples in their vicinity.

No mention of the promising features in teacher education would be complete without referring again to the vital importance of in-service training. The Cultural Missions, as travelling normal schools, are bridging the gap created by the lack of balance between teacher supply and demand. The school inspectors, through constant supervision in the field, are serving to counteract the deficiencies of untrained teachers and to co-ordinate the activities of the various school units. Even without taking into account the significance of their social-service functions, the missioners and inspectors form an indispensable cog in the machinery of teacher-training. Through their work a personnel problem that would otherwise appear discouraging is made hopeful and is being gradually solved.

The most heartening element in both teacher-training and Indian education is that the agencies used are strictly Mexican. This is stated with no intention of minimizing the advantages observed for similar institutions in other countries but rather with an appreciation of the fact that Mexicans are striving for their redemption in a Mexican way. The qualities which have made it possible for Mexicans to recognize their problems and to attempt to meet those problems in their own way can be depended on to go beyond the present level to even more fruitful stages. Mexican educators have been able to see the Mexican educational problem with astonishing clarity. They have begun their campaign for a cultural revolution by grounding the temples of education on Mexican soil and by building a Mexican institution from the ground up. The redemption of the Mexican masses has been placed in their own hands through institutions which are their institutions and by procedures which are not foreign to their environment or alien to their manner of life.

# CHAPTER VIII

# CHURCH, STATE, AND EDUCATION

IT is extremely unfortunate that, in contemplating the Church-State question in Mexico, the American people have no adequate criterion by which to judge the Mexican events which this conflict has brought to their attention. It would be easy to understand the feud between the civil power and the clergy were it not for the fact that the religious or spiritual functions of the latter becloud the issues and introduce complications that, in many respects, are irrelevant to the basic questions involved. Well-intentioned individuals and organizations in the United States, bemoaning the reported "religious persecutions," are attracted to the conflict between Church and State largely because of a spiritual bond of sympathy. Knowing only the American Catholic Church and having for a background only a knowledge of the healthy relations existing between the political State and the spiritual Church in the United States, these sympathizers cannot conceive of a State-Church controversy in which the religious aspects are merely incidental to a major question of State that is unrelated to the spiritual functions of the Church.

Religious freedom as known in this country has always been limited to freedom of worship and to spiritual independence. It has never gone beyond those boundaries which mark off political and economic provinces from those of religion. The Catholic Church in the United States has been, and is, an organization subject to the superior power of the State; its religious practices and policies are carried out on the same basis as those of any other organization within a democracy. If church organizations participate in the political and economic activities of the American society, they subject themselves to the same limitations, procedures, and possible penalties which face any one else. No one denies the supremacy of churches in the spiritual sphere. At the same time, it is generally agreed that when religious agencies branch out into temporal fields they thereby become subject to temporal measures. Questions of political and economic supremacy have never seriously threatened the pleasant relationships that have existed between any church and the American State. The province of the American Church has been, and is, a spiritual one. The cultural, social, economic, and political problems of the nation rest in the State and, in so far as a church is concerned in these latter problems, it is subject to State regulation and control. An eminent Mexican scholar, Alfonso Toro, has said:

I understand well that it is difficult for the people of the United States to understand that there are rogues who seek to cover their political purposes with religious cloaks. I understand and envy the United States that aspect. I know very well that there is not a single article in the American Constitution that deals with the religious question simply because, through the good fortune of that people, there has not been the necessity of including it in the Fundamental Charter. There all churches distinguish religious attitude and conduct from political interests and conduct; whereas, in our country, from the time of Independence to our day, intrusion of the Catholic Church in temporal and political affairs has been a constant historical problem with various aspects. . . . That intrusion is the sole reason for the constant weakness of spiritual influence that the Mexican Catholic Church has had over the years. . . . The majority of the Catholics in Mexico . . . make a perfect and clear distinction between their religious duties and their obedience to the temporal and political tendencies of their bad pastors.

The relationship between Church and State in Mexico is very different from that to which we, in the United States, have been accustomed. It is so different, in fact, that the Mexican Catholic Church might be considered as being unrelated to the American Catholic Church. Its history is different and the processes and procedures by which it has played its part in Mexican development are in direct contrast with those by which the same sect has established itself as a benevolent and religious organization in the United States. As a matter of fact, were it not for the universal religious doctrines of the Catholic Church, there would be no resemblance and no relationship between the American Church and the Mexican. For our purposes it is best to eliminate any consideration of religious doctrines or beliefs in order that we may be in a better position to judge the effects that the Church-State controversy has had on education in Mexico. I say this because of a firm conviction that religion, as such, is probably the most insignificant factor in the controversy. The conflict in Mexico has arisen because, unlike the American Church which is modern and in which religion is the chief concern, the Mexican Catholic Church is the medieval Church—the colonial Church which was both State and Church and which exercised not only a religious function but a political one in which economic power was essential to its existence.

The colonial Church of Mexico has been in a position of political and economic prominence for centuries. Jealous of that pre-eminence, it has failed to recognize the course of events that has raised Mexico from a provincial field of exploitation to a modern nation in which the democratic State is sovereign and to which all internal social and economic manifestations must be made subject. In spite of changed conditions, the Mexican clergy have sought to retain the privileges and advantages which they enjoyed in colonial days and have attempted to set the Church on a par with the State, refusing to subject their activities to the Supreme Law of a democratic commonwealth. The conflict in Mexico is not between religion and democracy. It is a clash between the sovereign power of the State and the power of a political and economic organization that threatened the very sovereignty of that State. The bone of contention is political and economic power, not religion.

## The State and the Clergy

The indictments that may be made against the Mexican clergy are not indictments against Catholicism and are not directed at the spiritual beliefs of Catholics, either in Mexico or elsewhere. Only an elimination of religion from this discussion can bring about true understanding of the real factors involved. Justification for this procedure can be found in the mass of documentary evidence that has been compiled to explain the events which have resulted from the enforcement of edicts by the State against the administrative practices of the Church. American readers will find a recent publication by the Attorney-General of the Republic, ex-President Emilio Portes Gil, of great interest in this connexion. Portes Gil, in *The Conflict between the Civil Power and the Clergy*, has set forth the historical and legal aspects of the Church question. Other references in the Bibliography abound with explanations and illustrations that support the contention that the Church, aside from its religious aspects, presented a menace to the sovereignty of the Mexican nation. It is significant that both American and Mexican students who have given serious thought to the problem have either discarded the religious element or have given it only minor importance. All evidence points to the soundness of this point of view and reduces an evaluation of the problem to the study of Mexican political science in which theological considerations play no important part.

No one will deny that the Mexican Church, as a social institution, has made a tremendous contribution to Mexican life. The great men and women of the Mexican Church—Gante, Quiroga, Zumárraga, Las Casas, Sahagún, Sister Juana Inez de la Cruz, etc.—have carved prominent niches for themselves in the hall of fame of Mexican history. Mexican civilization today is a monument to the stupendous efforts of pioneering churchmen who became martyrs to the cause of a nation in the making. The religious beliefs of the Catholic Church have added no little to the spiritual life of the masses, which could look to the Christian religion for the solace and consolation that would steel them against their miserable existence. The Catholic religion has formed a bright spot in the spiritual life of the oppressed Mexican masses. No one has any quarrel with this phase of the Church's work. The unfortunate thing is that, hand in hand with this laudable campaign of religious redemption, the temporal power of the Church paradoxically exploited in this world those whom it would save for the next. That, in essence, is the basic source of the puzzling situations by virtue of which a humanitarian religious sect finds itself embroiled in political and material manifestations in the lives of its converts.

The educational contributions of the Catholic Church have already been noted and extolled. What there was of education in Mexico previous to 1910 must be assigned largely to the credit of Church initiative and interest. In this connexion, as in the religious field, the Church has served Mexico well. The stand taken by some churchmen in behalf of the Mexican people speaks of a noble humanitarian interest. Leading figures in the Church, both Mexican and foreign, have at times raised their voices in behalf of the underprivileged in Mexico. From the first days of the Conquest on through the centuries, there have been those who, from within the Church, protested the material tendencies of the Mexican clergy and deplored the light in which these misguided prelates placed the Church.

Would that what has been said of the Church in education could be said of the part that this institution played in other phases of Mexican development. Even before the time of independence, the clergy were definitely aligned with those conservative forces which were most likely to continue the Church in its position of medieval power and prestige. When Hidalgo tried to stir his countrymen to rebellion against the reign of Spain, the Church was the first to impose its sanctions and penalties against him and his followers. The liberal movement which Hidalgo inaugurated was carried on in the face of excommunications that had been directed by the Church against all who lent him aid and assistance. Upon his capture, the Church withdrew the protection which his religious robes gave him and made it possible for his captors to execute him. Independence was achieved against the policies and wishes of the Church. The Catholic clergy aligned themselves with the *criollo* elements that rose to power when freedom from Spain was secured and bent every effort to thwart the accomplishment of those reforms for which independence had been sought by Mexicans. The Church gave its blessing to Iturbide during the first Empire. It opposed national defence during the American invasion of 1847 and covertly welcomed the Americans. No greater evidence of the antagonism that existed between the liberal forces in Mexico and the Church can be found than in the provisions included in the Constitution of 1857. At that time, when the liberal forces were able to muster sufficient strength, they ignored the Church in so far as possible and wrote into the Constitution ideas that looked towards the complete separation of Church and State. Mexican leaders of the time recognized that the political and economic dominance of the Church was an evil influence that was stunting the growth of independent Mexico and that had to be curbed if Mexico was to rise.

The loss of prestige suffered by the Church through the victory of the liberals in 1857 caused it to turn to continental Europe in its hopes for a return to prominence. It played an active part in promoting the negotiations which resulted in the movement by European nations to impose a foreign emperor on the Mexican people. The Church hoped that the ascension of the Austrian Archduke, Maximilian, to the throne of the Mexican Empire would return it to a position of major political influence. The Church frowned when that puppet of the diplomatic fates began to demonstrate a real and lively interest in the welfare of the people.

The fall of Maximilian was the result of the rebellion of the liberals in Mexico against practically the same conditions which had incited them to win independence from Spain. The first years of the restoration of the Mexican Republic saw the Church lose further ground in governmental affairs. Throughout this period, however, it did not cease to instigate the return of conservative government wherein it could retain some semblance of political control.

When Porfirio Díaz rose to the Presidency of the Republic, he was aided and abetted by the Catholic Church in flouting orderly and constitutional procedures. Through connivance with this ruthless dictator, who was unscrupulous in his use of its assistance, the Church was able to circumvent the legal principles which had been established by past liberal governments in the interests of the Mexican State. Whereas the Constitution expressly forbade the ownership of property by the Church, Díaz and the clergy entered into arrangements whereby third parties acted as figureheads in the possession of property that actually belonged to the Church. Other legal requirements, including those dealing with education, were either openly ignored or were circumvented by procedures of questionable legality and of bad faith. At all times the Church was acting in the capacity of a State within a State and was making every effort to fortify itself in that position. It acknowledged temporal allegiance and subservience only to the Vatican in Rome.

In reviewing the obstructionist policy that the Catholic Church has followed in Mexican national affairs, Dr. J. M. Puig Casauranc, then Secretary of Education, stated in 1926: "If the peace of our country and its institutions are thus placed in constant peril and if the Fatherland is placed in constant danger thereby, it would be stupid, it would be criminal that we should entrust to Catholic priests the formation of the concept of the Fatherland in our children."

In many respects the Church in Mexico has constituted itself a political party with extremely conservative political leanings and policies. It has financed revolts, has given moral support to minor and major rebellions, has participated in sedition against the government, and has displayed a material greed that is not only scandalous but that is most unworthy of the high religious ideals for which it stands. As a political power, supported by wealth that at times has reached fabulous proportions, it has always presented itself as a stumbling block to popular growth and nationalism. If it has suffered serious reverses in its political campaigns, it appears ridiculous for it to shirk the political responsibility of its acts by seeking to fall back on its religious role. The Church-State controversy in Mexico is a purely internal question of political and economic supremacy.

The nineteenth century definitely established the principle that the Church should no longer be a factor in the affairs of national government. The Church-State conflict which has broken out in recent years is one which was settled by constitutional provisions as early as 1857. This should be clearly understood. Though it was almost seventy years before these provisions were put into effect, during all that period there was ample opportunity to rectify any errors that may have been incorporated in the Constitution. It ill befits any organization to deny the validity of constitutional provisions which, though not rigidly enforced over a long period, have been in existence and subject to modification for more than three-quarters of a century. There are orderly processes by which the Constitution and Laws of the United Mexican States may be revised and reformed if such is the will of the people. Each time that such revisions have been made, the nation has repeated and strengthened the position which it has taken against clerical domination.

It is inevitable that the active part which the Church played in temporal affairs should have a direct bearing upon its relationship with the masses of the people. The Church was engaged in acquiring great wealth and in exploiting Mexican resources. To do this, it required the services of Mexican labour and placed itself in the same position as that of any other vested interest. A multiplication of churches and monasteries was achieved through the exploitation of the devout masses. The Church capitalized upon its control of Mexican consciences to such an extent that, for example, in Cholula, a town of less than 8,000 population, it was able to erect 365 temples—a church for each day of the year! The resources for such expansion came from Mexican soil. The buildings were constructed by Mexican labour. In all, the poverty-stricken, oppressed Mexican masses carried the enormous burden of a church's ambitions for temporal prominence. Assessments and contributions from the poor *pelados* financed the conspiracies and rebellions of the Church. Devout peasants gladly sacrificed themselves to the political Church. Fanatically faithful to religious tenets, they were led to shirk their duties and responsibilities as Mexican citizens and to become pawns in the worldly machinations of church administration.

## Education and the Church

The liberal thinkers of the nineteenth century soon realized that the Church could not be dislodged while it controlled the education of youth. With this in view, they sought to reduce the power of the Church by releasing the property which it held in mortmain and by specifying that primary education should be a non-religious education. The Constitutional reforms of the latter half of the nineteenth century showed great insight in seeking to relieve the misery of the Mexican people. The Church might well have subscribed to these reforms in the interest of popular welfare had it not been so concerned about its own temporal power. On the contrary, it made every effort to nullify these reforms and, in large part, succeeded in doing so during the Díaz regime.

The Revolution of 1910 found the clergy aligned with the forces against which the people were revolting. The Church had demonstrated its opposition to national welfare, had become an exploiting vested interest, and was one of the oppressors against whom the people rebelled. It had contributed to popular ignorance and misery through its campaign for material wealth and political domination and had to suffer the consequences of the victory of the masses.

The end of the Revolution found the people hungry for the fruits of learning. They knew the dangers which accompanied subservience to the educational functions of the Church, so they again sought to provide against a recurrence of Church control of popular thought. Article 3 of the Constitution of 1917 set forth that "Education shall be free, but that which is given in official educational establishments shall be *lay* as also shall be elementary and superior primary instruction that is imparted in private establishments." Other articles also sought to regulate Church-State relationships in other fields.

These safeguards against clerical domination of Mexican thought were not immediately enforced, owing to the still unsettled condition of the country. It remained for the Calles government, in 1926, to initiate the movement for the enforcement of these constitutional provisions. Immediately an uproar was raised by the Church and its supporters. The *Cristero* Revolution broke out and had to be suppressed. The clergy made every attempt to circumvent the intent of the laws and to handicap the efforts of the Secretariat of Education in regulating schools in accordance with the Constitution. In spite of the willingness of federal officials to arbitrate the procedures by which conformity to the Constitution was to be achieved, the Church retaliated by obstructionist measures. The position upheld by the revolutionary governments at all times has been that, while regulatory provisions might be softened and modified, they would not and could not under any circumstances arbitrate the mandates of the Constitution. Their function was to enforce the Constitution in as orderly a manner as possible but, above everything, they had to conform to the regulations included in the Fundamental Law, regardless of consequences.

It should be observed that the Constitution of 1917 did not prohibit the establishment of primary schools by religious organizations. Furthermore it made no mention of secondary, vocational, and advanced education. The Church was perfectly free to continue, even to expand, in the educational field provided that it subject its primary schools to the constitutional requirement that primary education be a lay education, free from religious influences and direction. This provision is an extreme application of a common principle in American education—the right and duty of the State to educate the children of the State *in the interests of the State*. The restrictions placed by Mexico on the nature of elementary education, however drastic they might be from the standpoint of religious instruction, are those to which the schools in the United States have conformed in principle. While Americans may regret that the Mexican Church has been deprived of this medium of religious education, there is no consistency in denying that the Mexican programme of federal schools is grounded on a sound principle of education in a democracy.

The comparative leniency of the 1917 Constitution did not satisfy the Church and it bent every effort to prevent the application of regulations intended to enforce compliance with Article 3. Popular demonstrations were stirred up against the federal programme. Manifestos and decrees were published and the people were urged to disobey and ignore their civic responsibilities. A pastoral letter signed by the Mexican bishops in 1926 stated: "As the law does not recognize the right of Catholic primary schools to impart the religious education to which they are obligated by their nature, we charge the consciences of the heads of families that they prevent their children from attending those educational plants where they will endanger their faith and good customs and where the texts violate the religious neutrality recognized by the Constitution itself."

The Catholic clergy were in open rebellion against the orderly processes of the government. They refused to recognize the mandates of the Constitution. Instead of taking recourse to the orderly procedures by which this document might be revised, they dedicated themselves to a campaign of conspiracy and sedition. Remnants of the forces which sought to shake the country through the unsuccessful *Cristero* Revolution continued to receive support and encouragement. Even today small groups of these rebels are to be found operating in various states, endangering the lives of federal employees and of those who are in sympathy with the new movement in education.

When interviewed by representatives of the American press in 1926, General Plutarco Elías Calles, President of Mexico, said: "I will ask you what can and what should the government of a country do when any association whatsoever, whether its tendencies be religious or otherwise, publicly refuses to acknowledge the Constitution, announces its intentions of fighting it, and incites the people to disobey it?" With equal insistence President Cárdenas stated on January 1, 1935: ". . . there is a marked and stupid connivance of foreign Catholic elements which, by utilizing an insidious propaganda against the educational activities which the National Government is putting into practice to free the Nation from blind clerical oppression, seek to mould American public opinion in order to alienate its sympathy from us and to close it against us. . . . On other occasions the Mexican Government has been able to show before the world and before the opinion of the American people that the social activities which are unfolded in Mexico are those of education and of economic liberation within the most justified desires of the human race and which, though they may appear exacting, are not comparable with the economic situation and the educational situation which the American people actually enjoy."

The natural result of Church opposition to the policies of the federal government was a consolidation of the forces which sympathized with the federal programme. Since the followers of the Church had devoted themselves to a campaign of obstruction and rebellion, it was a foregone conclusion that the forces in power would seek to strengthen their position as regards the Church question through constitutional reforms

which presented the only means for a nationalistic development. Article 3 of the Constitution of 1917 was again reformed
in the fall of 1934. On page 102 we have reproduced Article 3
as it was revised in 1934 and as it exists today. Instead of re-
ceding from the position of antagonism to religious education,
the revised Article went beyond the provisions of the Constitution of 1917 and specifically sought to eliminate any semblance of religious education from "primary, secondary, or
normal schools." This was the answer of the duly constituted
popular government to the challenge which had been thrown
in the face of the Mexican people by the clergy. Through
orderly procedures, the people again expressed themselves as
opposed to the point of view championed by the clergy.

The new educational movement in Mexico is bound by the
supreme law of the land to discard all elements that point to
the introduction of Church influences. The thesis upheld by
the Secretariat of Education is not a debatable one. The application of the mandates of Article 3—reflecting the will of the
Mexican people—is compulsory upon governmental agencies
sworn to support the Constitution. Any other course is dependent upon further reforms of the Constitution. Any different procedure must await the expression of the will of the
people through due process of constitutional amendment. It
has to be recognized that, no matter how just it may seem from
afar, any action that flaunts disobedience or sedition with respect to the expressed wish of the Mexican populace must be
wrong in Mexico. The autonomy of a democratic nation is
based upon the supremacy of the popular will as expressed
through the legal machinery which the people have established
for their own self-government. The Mexican Constitution has
tried to regulate the activities of the Church so that that organization may not interfere in the political and economic life
of the nation. To the extent that the Church will subject itself

to Mexican legal processes, to that extent it can become a part of Mexican life. As long as the Church does not confuse temporal affairs with spiritual functions it is not in conflict with the civil power of Mexico.

We have already described how education is an integral part of the functions of the Mexican government. This is particularly true of the Socialistic Schools that have been created and which are guided by the principles set forth in Article 3. Any controversy which affects governmental procedures in Mexico has an immediate effect upon the educational programme. The Socialistic School is placed in the very midst of any dispute between the State and the clergy. An illustration of this is found in the pastoral letter of January 1936. This letter, signed by the Mexican archbishops and bishops, makes an outspoken attack directly upon the government's schools. It urges parents to keep their children out of federal schools under penalty of committing a mortal sin.

The schools, as instrumentalities of national government, must play their part in upholding the course followed by the duly established administrative forces of the nation. The Church-State controversy looms big in the cultural revolution. Educational agencies must serve as the front line in the campaign against the attacks made upon constituted authority. The schools must act in their capacity as schools of the Revolution in defending the programme that has arisen from the Revolution and which, until changed by the people themselves, constitutes the will of the people of Mexico. Every school programme in Mexico shows some evidence of the efforts being made by the government to counteract clerical sedition and rebellion. Often an extreme picture is painted of the atrocities committed in the name of the Church and of the fanatical exploitation of the Mexican people. The "whispering campaign" against the Socialistic School is answered by the schools with a forceful though often rabid and extreme exposition of church evils.

## Need for Social Balance

It is to be regretted that elements on both sides of the controversy have gone to extremes in supporting their views. Over-zealous supporters of the federal programme have been parties to demonstrations and even crimes that besmirch the soundness of the position which they uphold. In combating religious fanaticism some educational agencies have in turn become fanatical against the actions of the Church and, in some instances, against religion itself. The unlawful activities of *Cristero* rebels have at times been answered in kind by radical constitutionalists. These deplorable manifestations, arising from the abnormal situation caused by internal dissension over the policies of government, do not represent or do credit to the issue at stake. The fundamental question is: Have the Mexican people, through their Constitution and laws, the power to regulate the internal affairs of the nation? There can be only one answer to such a question.

The practice of the Catholic religion is not prohibited in Mexico by the federal Constitution or laws. Religious worship is still a personal right and the exercise of that right should not be confused with the regulatory and preventive measures taken by the national government to ensure itself against the inroads of an organization that would set itself up as a State within a State. Extra-legal "persecutions" of Catholics in Mexico have, in all probability, occurred. Equally unwarranted activities on the part of Church supporters have brought on some of these "persecutions." These are incidental to the main issue and are beside the point in an evaluation of the conflict between the civil power and the clergy. They do not justify a condemnation of the federal policy nor do they outweigh the basic reasons which justify that policy.

The bitter warfare observed in the development of a cultural revolution is bound to continue for some time to come. It is to be hoped that soon the clergy and federal agencies will arrive at an understanding and an acceptance of the part that each must play in the interest of the Mexican people. It might well be predicted that, to the extent that federal agencies enter into a criticism or opposition of religious ideas, to that extent the federal government is placing itself in the same position for which it has criticized the Church. As long as the Mexican government limits its opposition to the Church to the question of political autonomy it is marching on safe ground for which it has authoritative precedents in history. Intrusion into religious fields can be of little value to the federal programme. This caution is fairly well observed by educational leaders. In a like manner, it is to be hoped that the Church will recognize the justice of the policy whereby the federal government is seeking to retain temporal sovereignty in Mexico.

I would venture to say that the day is not far off when such a healthy state of affairs may be observed in the United Mexican States. Already one may note evidences of a trend in that direction. In spite of laws limiting the number of priests and restricting certain forms of religious practices, both governmental officials and the population in general are permitting informal arrangements which do not seriously impair the victory attained in separating State and Church. It appears that gradually an agreement will be reached whereby religion will be given full sway through legal and orderly outlets and in a manner which does not challenge the supremacy of the State. Such a condition would prove a great benefit to the educational programme. No longer would schools have to be concerned with metaphysical gymnastics which are now thought necessary in order to give children a satisfactory point of view. The time now devoted to the study of such problems could well be employed in more useful learning. This does not mean that the schools should gloss over those pages of history in which the Church is placed in a bad light by her past actions. Sound civic points of view as well as a proper appreciation of the benefits of a Christian religion, unhampered by material aspects, cannot but be of value to the coming generations. But there is grave danger in allowing political clashes to become so prominent in education that an otherwise scientific point of view may be warped into negative attitudes in the spiritual life of pupils.

The Church question mars the promising picture of Mexican cultural renascence. Without reference to political right or wrong, the Church-State conflict is a drawback to Mexican progress and a handicap in the search for social balance. While, for purposes of analysis, the spiritual factor should be eliminated from an evaluation of the conflict, this factor will inevitably have its effect upon the mental reactions of the masses of the people. The religious element is bound to confuse the real issues, creating a situation which will have undesirable effects upon the total programme of the peaceful revolution. Political justice lies with the government but it is regrettable that the cultural values of Christianity must be denied more ample sway in the educational awakening sponsored through the new schools. The belief might also be expressed that the Mexican clergy are unwise in permitting temporal means to stand in the way of the redemption of the Mexicans—the one common ground upon which Church and State might meet in discharging their respective responsibilities.

*To Educate Is to Redeem*

# CHAPTER IX

# EDUCAR ES REDIMIR

T HE Mexican scene has changed. Long years of struggling have at last brought peace to a war-weary people. The feudal walls of cultural isolation are breaking down before the onslaught of a changing social order. Geographic barriers have been penetrated by the energetic efforts of modern forces and by the desire of the Mexican people to widen their horizons. The isolated streams of diverse cultures, arising in a variety of settings, are becoming tributaries to the tide of nationalism and are adding their force to the current of Mexican progress—tingeing the flow with native colours.

There is a changed point of view in the administration of Mexican affairs and in the relationships between social classes. For centuries the Mexican peoples were *"los de abajo,"* the underdogs—to be governed, exploited, and controlled at the will of those in power. The masses of the people were mere pawns in the game played by political and economic forces. Physically and culturally far removed from the governing aristocracy, the great majority of the Mexican peoples were manipulated by those whom the turn of circumstance had placed in the role of *patrón, militar, cura,* or *político.* The *campesino* gave everything, receiving nothing. He fought the battles of ephemeral causes for the leaders of the moment. Why? *Quién sabe!* Maybe because he was happier fighting for a cause, ephemeral as it might be, than dwelling in traditional pauperism, forlornly brooding on a hopeless existence. But the pendulum has swung and positions have been reversed. By virtue of a revolution, the people have risen to power. They have achieved the control that heretofore rested in the hands of a few. Government now must needs reflect popular will and respond to the needs of the proletariat.

It is indeed surprising to speak of popular government in Mexico as something that has just arisen. Theoretically Mexico has been a democratic nation for more than a hundred years. Nevertheless, democracy has existed in name only, with little semblance of nationalism or of general popular participation in the making of governmental policies. A State in which the people did not participate in government could not be expected to respond to popular needs. The rebellion of the masses against their institutions is in itself evidence of the disregard in which the government held the problems of the masses and, conversely, it reflects the intolerance of the people for a government that did not represent the majority of Mexicans. The Revolution of 1910 demonstrated that the people would no longer stand for governmental neglect and indifference. It showed that Mexicans would no longer tolerate capitalistic exploitation on the part of the interests which dominated the government. The Revolution went still further. It warned future governments that the Mexican peoples expected to be freed from economic subjugation and cultural isolation. It showed that Mexicans were not only eager to receive those privileges which, in the past, had been reserved for the small group constituted as the upper classes but that they would resort to civil war to obtain them.

The major achievement of the Revolution is a changed point of view. Whereas the view of the past might be described as having been capitalistic—the profit of the few—today it is characterized by its concern for the popular welfare. The Mexican has forced a social point of view upon his government. It is true that he has gained lands, a general improvement in labour conditions, and a number of changes in the material aspects of his life. But he has gained more than just that. He has become free, whereas before he lived in semi-slavery. He can now look forward to the promise of the future, whereas in the past he was virtually without hope. He may still be poor; he may still have to earn a meagre existence in the midst of the rigours of a backward economic order. His material existence may not be greatly improved over what he experienced in the past but today he is subject to possible redemption, whereas before he was consigned to almost perpetual neglect.

No one aspect of Mexico is more characteristic of the changed order than the fresh movement in education. The very corner-stone of the new social order is the ideal that through education the Mexican can be and will be redeemed. *"Educar es redimir"*—"To educate is to redeem." The cultural revolution is the *sine qua non* of the reforms which were the battle cries in the Revolution of 1910. The school is the agency through which the fertile masses are being cultivated so that the social and economic reforms which the people demanded may be established. It is little wonder that the new schools have become socialistic schools. It is their function to socialize the contrasting people into the trend of a popular nationalism. It is their responsibility to mould together the clashing cultures of the nation and to facilitate the development of a social whole out of the many small social entities that had existed heretofore as feudal *haciendas*, towns and hamlets, states and regions. The Socialistic School is to place the fundamental tools of learning in the hands of the people, guiding their first steps in the part which they must play in the political, social, and economic processes of the Mexican nation. It is the school's task to take the newly born Mexican proletariat and instruct it in the curriculum of an active national life. The new schools of old Mexico are more than classrooms of academic preparation. Through the schools the people of Mexico seek to redeem themselves by an education that meets their needs and aspirations.

The new schools have concentrated their attention upon rural problems. They have laid their roots in the realities which are presented by the Mexican scene. They have espoused the cause of the vast majority of the people of the nation, have dedicated their efforts to the solution of the immediate problems which confront Mexico. In an age when the educative process has acquired a polish never before known and when the goals of education in other lands are obscured by complicated methodology, terminology, and ideology, Mexico has chosen to take a direct path towards the achievement of its aims. The schools are making use of the materials at hand in order that, by such use, those very materials might be improved.

The rural school in Mexico is not a polished institution. It is rural in terms of the total rurality of Mexicans. It is poor, financially, and is probably inefficiently manned. There is, in effect, much room for improvement in the educational programme inaugurated by the federal government in 1921 and which we now observe in full swing. In the face of all such criticisms, it cannot be denied that the Mexican approach to their social and educational problems is sound. The Socialistic School may be criticized on several grounds, but the charge cannot be made that it is not a popular school or that it has failed to reflect the cultural and social needs of the Mexican people.

The present educational movement in Mexico is still in an experimental stage. It is still on trial as an effective means of nationalizing and socializing the contrasting peoples of Mexico in their several environments. It should be kept clearly in mind that the Socialistic School is a school of the Revolution —that its procedures are those which can be used with profit by the prime agency of a cultural revolution. Each school changes with its milieu and the pace of progress is adapted to the capacities of the school's patrons. Many of the accomplishments of the new schools are still in the future and the effectiveness of the new programme must be weighed in the balance of time. There are many problems within the scope of the educational programme that still remain unsolved. Health conditions present a challenge to the efficacy of reform through education. Great portions of the population are still illiterate. The place of women in the social, cultural, and economic scale is yet far from satisfactory. Alcoholism still spreads its enervating tentacles over the untutored masses. The problems arising from the economic upheavals of the agrarian revolution and of labour reforms present a continuing demand upon the powers of a social education. Indeed, the work of the schools has just begun.

There are many obstacles to the successful attainment of the ends of redemption through education, but the Mexican mêlée has ended and the nation is embarked upon its campaign with purpose and direction. The federal programme of education represents the spearhead of the current which has shot out from the whirlpool of the mêlée. There are forces which seek to draw this current back upon itself, nullifying the victory already achieved. The insistent opposition of the Mexican clergy constantly threatens to obstruct the course of social education in the Mexican democracy. This group, confusing national welfare with its own pre-eminence and privilege, constitutes a source of danger to the agencies which the people of Mexico have established as the means by which they will redeem themselves. Other problems of lesser significance still worry those who have charge of directing education. In spite of forebodings that may arise because of these problems, the Mexican school rests secure in the knowledge that it is a school of the people and that the people of Mexico have supported it in the past and still continue to receive it as their own. Before such manifestations of popular approval, the thrusts of a discontented clergy or of other dissenting influences cannot hope to prevail.

Wherein has the Mexican scene changed? Is it not true that Mexicans have seen other times when a lull in the storm of revolt has given promise of permanent peace, only to bring disappointment when the turmoil broke forth anew? There have been other occasions when it appeared that Mexico was on a safe and sane road to national recovery, always with the same result—a return to the mêlée. The fleeting periods of comparative peace have always been followed by the scourge of civil war characterized by governmental instability, economic insecurity, and spiritual privation. It would seem that Mexicans were doomed to a fatalistic course of events wherein social security is but a flickering mirage, ever beyond reach. Is there any assurance that Mexico has outlived her baleful heritage? In what fundamental way does the governmental programme of the "men of the Revolution" differ from the unsuccessful attempts of the past?

The present nationalistic movement has cast its lot with a fresh philosophy, an ideal new to Mexico. The experiences of a tumultuous history have been turned to profit and a popular regime seeks peace in revolution. In the present revolution, as in the past, the surging masses are the means but, unlike the past, they are also the ends. The battles fought are social ones; the weapons are social agencies. Rebellious against the elements that made them strangers in their own land, Mexicans are attacking the shackles of ignorance and privation by waging a war in peace. They have commandeered the educational agencies of the nation and have set them to the task of a cultural revolution. The schools of the Republic are treading the path of popular reform, carrying enlightened hope to forgotten Mexico.

The change that has come over Mexico is spiritual. No longer are Mexican hearts weighed down by the despair and loneliness bred of traditional spiritual poverty. The faint ray of hope that for centuries has presaged the break of a new day now shines in the dawn that is Mexican emancipation. No longer need the lowly *peón* gaze towards a horizon darkened by the gloomy clouds of slavery and of cultural isolation. The miserable *pelado* is no richer, but he is free—free to hope and dream and work, free to seek his salvation from the misery of his condition. He is free to grasp the outstretched hand of his comrades who, in seeking redemption for themselves, have learned the virtues of co-operation and have taken up the task of social reconstruction. The despised *indio,* astounded by the turn of events that has cast him up from the dismal depths of slavery to the sunshine of democratic privilege, girds his loins against the trials of the future, sadder but wiser by the tortures suffered in the past. The thunder that rolled so frequently over Mexico, leaving the people trembling and exhausted, has been dispersed by a popular triumph.

The people have tasted the fruits of knowledge, they are learning the fundamentals of economic security and of social justice. The party that is in national power today may fall, and new prophets may arise to guide national destiny. Yet no one can take away what the masses of the people have already learned. New national administrations or parties must bow to the momentum created by the campaign of redemption through education which the new schools have inaugurated. Mexicans have placed their hope in a militant cultural renascence. They are conducting a revolution not by violence but by education. What they have learned so far convinces them that *Educar es redimir.*

GUERRERO

# RURAL SCENES

MORELOS

TARAHUMARAS,
CHIHUAHUA

INDIANS

HUICHOLES,
ZACATECAS

# PUBLIC MARKETS

### QUERÉTARO

LACQUER WORK, MICHOACÁN

# ARTS AND CRAFTS

POTTERY, JALISCO

TANNINO

# VILLAGE TRADES

### AGUASCALIENTES

POTTERY

MISSION ON WHEELS, ZACATECAS

# SCHOOL AND COMMUNITY

PEASANT BAND, OAXACA

TEACHERS LEARNING REGIONAL DANCE

# MISSIONERS AT WORK

TRANSPORTING WATER WHEEL

RURAL TEACHERS AT MISSION INSTITUTE

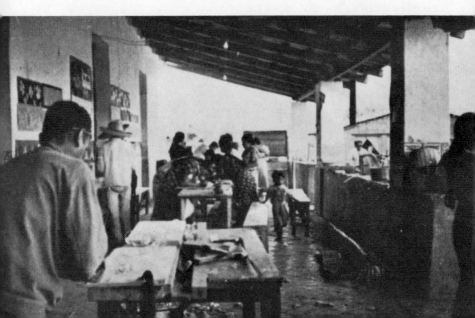

OAXACA

# FEDERAL RURAL SCHOOLS

TABASCO

SCHOOL OF ARTICLE 123, CHIHUAHUA

# LOCAL RESPONSIBILITY IN SCHOOL BUILDING

SCHOOL BUILT BY PEASANTS, ZACATECAS

COMMUNITY PARK

# SCHOOL "ANNEXES"

### PUEBLA

PIGEONS, CHICKENS, RABBITS, BEES

## AT AN *INTERNADO*

ZONGOZOTLA, PUEBLA

CLEANLINESS COMMITTEE

INDIAN STUDENTS

DOMESTIC SCIENCE

SHOP AT A BOARDING SCHOOL

# SCHOOL ACTIVITIES

A RURAL SCHOOL'S FRUIT AND VEGETABLE PLOT

# SCHOOL GARDENS

## TABASCO

EDUCAR ES REDIMIR

# GLOSSARY

VOWELS: *a* as in f*a*ther
    *e* " " sl*ei*gh
    *i* " " mach*i*ne
    *o* " " b*o*ught
    *u* " " r*u*le

CONSONANTS approximately as in English with the following exceptions:
    *c* before *e* or *i*, as *s*
    *g* " " " " " a strongly aspirated *h*
    *h* always silent
    *j* as a strongly aspirated *h*
    *ll* " *y*
    *ñ* " *ny* in ca*ny*on
    *qu* " *k*
    *z* " *s*

STRESS, in words ending with a vowel or with the letter *n* or *s*, falls on the next to the last syllable; in words ending with any other letter, the stress falls on the last syllable. Any departure from this rule is indicated by an acute accent on the irregularly stressed syllable (e.g., *gachupín, indígena.*)

PLURALS of nouns are formed by the addition to the singular of the suffixes (*s* or *es*).

*anexo*(*s*), annex; the playgrounds, open-air theatres, shops, co-operative stores, gardens, etc., which are established by and are a part of the schools' daily activities.

*barranca*(*s*), ravine; gorge.

*cacique*(*s*), Indian chief; political leader; chief.

*campesino*(*s*), peasant; countryman; the common people in rural Mexico.

*casa del pueblo*, house of the people. The first schools opened under the new movement in education were known, both popularly and officially, by this name. The phrase has a sentimental and sociological connotation not easily obtained from the literal translation.

*centavo*(*s*), cent; hundredth part of a peso.

193

*chile(s)*, chilli; red pepper.

*compañero(s)*, companion; friend.

*condueñazgo(s)*, common ownership; a farm or plantation owned jointly by several families.

*conquistador(es)*, conqueror. Used commonly in reference to the Spanish soldiers of fortune who settled New Spain, particularly those who came to the New World in the sixteenth century.

*criollo(s)*, creole; Mexican-born Spaniard (not to be confused with *mestizo* or half-breed, as *criollo* refers only to those of full European, white descent). See *peninsular* and *gachupín*.

*Cristero(s)*, follower of Christ; referring specifically to the religious insurgents who rebelled against the Mexican government during the *Cristero* Revolution of 1929 and who are still to be found, as small rebel bands, in many parts of Mexico.

*cura(s)*, parish priest; parson; clergyman.

*dotación(es)*, dowry; endowment, usually in the form of lands, made by the government to those whom it wishes to assist in their economic (agricultural) status.

*educar es gobernar*, to educate is to govern.

*educar es redimir*, to educate is to redeem.

*ejidatario(s)*, member of a community which owns an *ejido* (communal land grant).

*ejido(s)*, communal land grant. The land in such a grant is owned in common by the community. Tracts or "parcels" of land in the grant are assigned to individual adult members to be used indefinitely, usually until such a time as the tract is abandoned or given up voluntarily or until a redistribution is made by the community land council.

*encomienda(s)*, commandery; manorial guardianship. By authority of the Crown of Spain, Indians (and often their lands) were placed as wards of some (white) landowner or soldier who was in the government's good graces. These guardianships were known as *encomiendas* and were originally intended to bring about the rehabilitation and conversion of the Indians—the guardian being repaid for his trouble by the labour of the Indians. This practice immediately degenerated into a form of gross exploitation wherein whole Indian communities were bartered and held in virtual slavery.

*escuela(s) secundaria(s)*, secondary school (grades 7, 8, and 9).

*escuelas de peor es nada*, schools that are little better than nothing at all. Popular expression used in referring to the "rudimentary" (primary) schools established during 1911–1920.

*explotadores*, the exploiters. Commonly used in reference to the capital-

ists or to those who, though not capitalists in a true sense, profit at
the expense of the proletariat.

*fiesta(s)*, festival; feast; celebration.

*gachupín(es)*, Spaniard; popular term (somewhat derogatory) used to
designate a European Spaniard who settles in Mexico.

*grito de Dolores*, cry of independence by Father Hidalgo in 1810; literally, "shout of Dolores." Hidalgo raised the cry to arms at the
village of Dolores, Guanajuato, early in the morning of September
16, 1810.

*hacendado(s)*, plantation owner; large landholder.

*hacienda(s)*, plantation; large ranch; landed property. Refers to large
private landholdings.

*henequén*, sisal hemp; *Agave sisalana*. A fibrous plant, cultivated exten-
sively in Yucatán, which is the source of much of the wealth in that
state.

*huarache(s)*, sandal; Indian footwear varying in construction from crude
soles, held onto the feet by thongs, to intricately interwoven shoes
of great comfort and durability.

*indio(s)*, an Indian.

*insurgente(s)*, an insurgent; a rebel.

*internado(s)*, residence (boarding) school. Used to designate the federal
boarding schools for Indians.

*internado indígena*, Indian residence school. See *internado*.

*liga(s)*, alliance; league or federation; coalition; labour organization or
union. Various labour groups in Mexico are organized as *ligas*. See
*sindicato*.

*los de abajo*, those below; the masses; the downtrodden. Common phrase
for "the underdogs." Used as the title of a Mexican novel of the
Revolution, very similar to (but appearing several years before)
*All Quiet on the Western Front*.

*machete(s)*, cutlass; cane- or brush-knife. An all-purpose large knife
ranging in length from 18 to 36 inches and usually 2 to 3 inches
wide.

*maguey(es)*, agave; century plant. The juice from the various types of
*maguey* produces *pulque, mezcal*, and *tequila* (alcoholic beverages).
The leaves of the *pulque maguey* are often 6 feet in length.

*mesa central*, central tableland; high central plateau; the plateau between
the eastern and western mountain ranges or Sierras extending from
the border of the United States to the Isthmus of Tehuantepec. At
Mexico City the plateau rises 7,000 to 8,000 feet above sea level,
gradually sloping almost to sea level in the south and to 3,800 feet
above sea level at El Paso on the United States border.

*mestizaje(s)*, mixture of races.

*mestizo(s)*, Spanish-Indian half-breed; hybrid. Originally used to class the children whose fathers were Spanish and whose mothers were Indian. Later interbreeding among *mestizos*, whites, and Indians (and some Negroes) produced race mixtures variously classified but now known under the general term of *mestizos*.

*mejicano(s)*, Mexican; Aztec. The true *mejicano* is the Aztec, the original conqueror of the Valley of Mexico. The term has two general uses—to refer to the Aztec race (people, language, etc.) and to designate the nationals of Mexico. In the latter sense, it is incorrect to speak a "Mexican language," as the national language is Spanish.

*mezcal(es)*, species of maguey; the brandy distilled from the fermented juice of the *mezcal* plant.

*militar(es)*, soldier; military man.

*misionero(s)*, missioner; missionary. Now commonly used without any religious connotation; that is, a *misionero* is an educational missionary. The term refers specifically to the supervisor-teachers of 1921–1925 and to the members of the Cultural Missions.

*misionero pintor*, missioner-painter; the instructor in plastic arts in a Cultural Mission.

*nahuyaca(s)*, a vicious and deadly viper found in southern Mexico.

*normales ambulantes*, travelling normal schools. Phrase describing the Cultural Missions in one phase of their work—teacher-training.

*normalista(s)*, teacher who has been trained in a normal school; one who has completed the normal-school courses.

*patrón(es)*, landlord; patron; "the boss."

*pelado(s)*, penniless one; literally, a "shorn one." Derogatory term describing poverty-stricken individuals or groups. It implies cultural poverty and is sometimes used to express general contempt of any one, rich or poor.

*peninsular(es)*, peninsular; a Spaniard born on the Iberian Peninsula (Spain). *Peninsular*—a Spaniard born in Spain; *criollo*—a Spaniard born in Mexico. See *gachupin* and *criollo*.

*peón(es)*, common day-labourer.

*peso(s)*, the Mexican dollar. The value of the peso, like other national monetary units, varies in international exchange. Since November 1933, the Mexican government has stabilized the value of the peso in terms of the dollar at a ratio of 3.60 to one (one dollar equals 3.6 pesos; or one peso equals .28 of a dollar).

*pinole*, cereal powder. A very nutritive corn-meal powder used by the Tarahumara Indians. Tasty and palatable when mixed with water or milk. Has been sold commercially as a breakfast food in the United States.

*político(s)*, politician. This word is not very often used in a derogatory sense.

*posole*, a sort of gruel, consisting of a mixture of a corn-meal paste and water, used by the natives of south-eastern Mexico. As used in this volume, the term is not to be confused with the *posole* of central and northern Mexico which is a more elaborate dish with hominy-corn as the base.

*primaria(s)*, primary (school). The Mexican primary school extends over 6 years or grades—grades 1–4 inclusive are the "elementary-primary" and grades 5 and 6 are the "superior-primary" divisions of the school.

*pulque*, the milk-like wine obtained from the *pulque maguey* plant. The juice of the maguey is allowed to collect in a hollowed-out depression in the core of the plant. This juice is removed periodically and allowed to ferment in pigskin bags. The great ease with which *pulque* is prepared has spread its use tremendously and, while only mildly intoxicating, it is used constantly and in such large quantities that serious sociological problems have arisen because of its widespread use by the lower classes. Regulations and campaigns are being directed to control its use.

*pulquería(s)*, saloon; tavern, or wineshop, where pulque is sold.

*quién sabe*, literally, "who knows!" Phrase expressing general uncertainty or doubt.

*ranchería(s)*, community settlement composed of small farms.

*razas de bronce*, bronze races; also the races of bronze. Mexican Indians, particularly in central and southern Mexico, as distinguished from the "red" Indians of the north.

*revolucionario(s)*, revolutionist; a revolutionary. The term refers more specifically to those who took part in, or who believe in the ideals of, the Revolution of 1910.

*sindicato(s)*, labour organization; labour union. See *liga*.

*socórrame, en el nombre de Dios*, help me in the name of God. Common plea of the street beggars.

*tamal(es)*, a corn-meal, chilli, and meat roll wrapped (and boiled) in corn husks (in banana leaves in the tropics). Widely used over all of Mexico and variously prepared, but typically the staple dish of the Totonacs.

*tata*, term of reverence and endearment used for the father or grandfather or for one whom the speaker accepts, figuratively, in that affectionate relationship.

*tequila*, the highly intoxicating brandy distilled from the *tequila maguey* plant. See *pulque, mezcal*, and *maguey*.

*tierra y libertad*, land and liberty. The battle cry of the Mexican revolutionary, Emiliano Zapata, who rebelled against the agrarian practices of the old order. The phrase is now commonly used as the slogan of the peaceful agrarian revolution.

*zarape(s)*, blanket woven by the natives; men's shawl.

# SELECTED BIBLIOGRAPHY

Unpublished manuscripts, addresses, and the like have proved of great value in this study but, because of their nature, are not listed here. Mexican educators have been most kind in permitting the use of many studies, records, and reports which also cannot be listed as bibliographical references. I am particularly indebted to Professor Rafael Ramírez for the mass of material which he has made available to me and for his valuable suggestions and comments.

Reference to books written in English has been limited to the studies made by Cook, Gruening, Priestley, and Tannenbaum (American authors) and to those by Portes Gil and Teja Zabre (Mexican authors). Both Gruening and Priestley offer comprehensive bibliographies.

CÁRDENAS, LÁZARO. *Mensaje para 1935.* Mexico, Imprenta Mundial, 1935. 33 p.

CASTAÑEDA, CARLOS E. *Nuevos Documentos . . . Para la Historia de México.* Mexico, Talleres Gráficos de la Nación, 1929. Vol. II, 215 p.

CHÁVEZ, EZEQUIEL A. *Fray Pedro de Gante.* Mexico, Imprenta Mundial, 1934. 106 p.

CONTRERAS, ADOLFO. *Las Cooperativas y la Escuela Rural.* Mexico, Talleres Gráficos de la Nación, 1933. 96 p.

COOK, KATHERINE M. *The House of the People.* Washington, United States Government Printing Office, 1932. 72 p.

GRUENING, ERNEST. *Mexico and Its Heritage.* New York, D. Appleton-Century Co., 1928. 728 p.

GUTIÉRREZ OLIVEROS, ANTONIO. *La Escuela Primaria desde el Punto de Vista Social.* Mexico, Talleres Gráficos de la Penitenciaría del D.F., 1934. 19 p.

LERDO DE TEJADA, C. TREJO. *La Educación Socialista.* Mexico, Partido Nacional Revolucionario, 1935. 270 p.

MENDIZÁBAL, MIGUEL O. DE. *Civilizaciones Aborígenes Americanas.* Mexico, Museo Nacional, 1924. 347 p.

MEXICO. *Constitución Política de los Estados Unidos Mexicanos.* Mexico, Talleres Gráficos de la Nación, 1934 edition. 159 p.

MOLINA ENRÍQUEZ, ANDRÉS. *La Revolución Agraria en México*. Mexico, Talleres Gráficos del Museo Nacional de Arqueología, Historia y Etnografía, 1932. Books 1–4, about 165 p. each.

PARTIDO NACIONAL REVOLUCIONARIO. *La Cuestión Agraria Mexicana*. Mexico, Talleres Gráficos de la Cámara de Diputados, 1934. 321 p.

PORTES GIL, EMILIO. *The Conflict between the Civil Power and the Clergy*. Translated from Spanish. Mexico, Press of the Ministry of Foreign Affairs, 1935. 135 p.

PRIESTLEY, HERBERT. *The Mexican Nation*. New York, The Macmillan Co., 1923. 507 p.

PUIG CASAURANC, J. M. Educación Rural. *Publicaciones de la Secretaría de Educación Pública*; Tomo XVII, Num. 5. Mexico, Talleres Gráficos de la Nación, 1928. 27 p. Other articles by Puig are to be found in this series of bulletins.

SAENZ, MOISÉS. La Educación Rural en México. *Publicaciones de la Secretaría de Educación Pública*; Tomo XIX, Num. 20. Mexico, Talleres Gráficos de la Nación, 1928. 28 p. Other studies and reports by Saenz are to be found in this series of bulletins.

SÁNCHEZ PONTÓN, LUÍS. *Hacia la Escuela Socialista*. Mexico, Editorial Patria, 1935. 278 p.

SECRETARÍA DE LA ECONOMÍA NACIONAL. *México en Cifras (Atlas Estadístico)*. Mexico, Secretaría de la Economía Nacional, 1934. (Statistical Charts, 12″ x 18″); 90 p.

SECRETARÍA DE EDUCACIÓN PÚBLICA.
*El Esfuerzo Educativo en México (1924–1928)*. Mexico, 1929. Vol. I, 743 p.; Vol. II, 542 p.
*La Casa del Estudiante Indígena*. Mexico, 1927. 164 p.
*Las Misiones Culturales, 1932–1933*. Mexico, 1933. 357 p.
*Memoria*: Mexico, 1933, 1934, 1935; comprehensive report, published yearly, in four volumes of about 600 p. each.
*Plan de Acción de la Escuela Primaria Socialista*. Mexico, 1935. 46 p.
*Programa de Educación Pública para 1935*. Mexico, 1935. 30 p.
*Programas para las Escuelas Normales Rurales*. Mexico, 1933. 19 p.
Other pertinent references may be found in: *Biblioteca del Maestro Rural* (series of teachers' handbooks and manuals); *El Maestro Rural* (monthly magazine); *El Martillo* (pictorial newspaper); *Publicaciones de la Secretaría de Educación Pública* (series of departmental bulletins); and in the Secretariat's reports of educational conferences, particularly those of the Institute of Socialistic Orientation.

TANNENBAUM, FRANK. *Peace by Revolution*. New York, Columbia University Press, 1935. 317 p.

TEJA ZABRE, ALFONSO. *Guide to the History of Mexico*. Translated from the Spanish by P. M. Del Campo. Mexico, Press of the Ministry of Foreign Affairs, 1935. 375 p.

TORO, ALFONSO. *La Iglesia y el Estado en México*. Mexico, Talleres Gráficos de la Nación, 1927. 501 p.

ZEPEDA, RINCÓN, TOMÁS. *La Instrucción Pública en la Nueva España en el Siglo XVI*. Mexico, Universidad Nacional de México, 1933. 133 p.

ZOLLINGER, EDWIN. *Enrique C. Rébsamen*. Translated from German by Solomon Kahan. Mexico, Secretaría de Educación Pública, 1935. 100 p.

# INDEX

## DATE DUE

| | | | |
|---|---|---|---|
| APR 1 0 1980 | | | |
| APR 1 0 1981 | | | |
| APR 9 1981 | | | |
| | | | |
| NOV 4 1982 | | | |
| NOV 2 5 1982 | | | |
| 12-7-82 | | | |
| APR 1 0 1990 | | | |
| APR 2 2 2011 | | | |
| | | | |
| | | | |
| | | | |
| | | | |
| | | | |
| | | | |
| | | | |